# Floral Folklore

## THE FORGOTTEN TALES BEHIND
## NATURE'S MOST ENCHANTING PLANTS

### Alison Davies

ILLUSTRATIONS BY SARAH WILDLING
FOREWORD BY ANNA POTTER

*Leaping Hare Press*

# CONTENTS

# FOREWORD

*Clutching the smushed Rose petals in my hand, grass stains all over my pale denim knees, I knew I was in for it. There would be shouting about washing, and about the mess and destruction made in Nana's Rose garden. And that's before they found the empty bottles of expensive body lotions and perfumes that I'd emptied in order to house my creations. But it was worth it. . . . the scent of my homemade garden potion perfume was far superior to the fake staleness of the wretched stuff the fancy sales lady used to come around with.*

This deeply intrinsic call to nature is a key value that I share with Alison, the author of this book. Acts such as breathing deeply after brushing past the Geraniums or tasting the bittersweet Magnolia leaves from a neighboring garden are the very things that many of us need as an antidote to our fast-paced, quick fix, consumer-led society.

The pages of this book offer tales that were once passed from generation to generation, around a fire or a dinner table: tales of practices that were once a central part of seasonal living, but that have somehow become lost in the digital ether. Following the seasons, each chapter will (re)introduce you to the stories behind many familiar flowers, offering a deeper insight into their origins, and exploring the myths and meanings associated with each one. Dark tales of the underworld, poisonous perils, and magic feature alongside lighter stories of hope and friendship in this book. Reading each story, I'm reminded, as I often feel at sunset or when the sun shines on snow covered trees, that the ancient ways must not be forgotten, and should be protected at all costs, for within them lies the medicine that soothes and restores human weariness, and plugs us back into the vastness of universal wisdom and beauty.

Alongside the hidden tale behind each flower, this book also offers practical ways in which you can create a ritual or mindful practice to strengthen the connection between yourself and each plant and season. By getting closer to nature and its rhythms, you can gain a deeper connection to your own inner seasons and processes, and activities such as songs, games, crafts, cooking, and meditation—all featured in this book—can help reconnect you with the web of the natural world.

Whenever I'm arranging the flowers from this book, I will hold their tales close, weaving their stories of sadness and joy to aid the act of expressing feeling through each flower. I can imagine summer walks through gardens, reciting these tales to my children, and to their children. I have found it so insightful for my own practice to reflect and spend more focused time getting to know the beautiful selection of flowers and plants in this book, and I hope you will too.

Anna Potter
*Author of* Flower Philosophy *and* The Flower Fix,
*founder of Swallows & Damsons*

# INTRODUCTION

## THE SIGNIFICANCE OF THE NATURAL WORLD

Everything you do, even the ebb and flow of your breathing, comes from nature. Your connection with the natural world is inherent to who you are. It drives you to evolve and flourish within your environment, to form lifelong connections, and to create a sense of place and purpose.

The fascination we have for our surroundings runs deep, because ultimately we are one and the same with the earth that sustains us. The land made us, and it continues to shape us. Our ancestors understood this. They recognized the power of the natural realm and worked with it to secure a bountiful future: foraging and ploughing the land; sewing seeds; tending crops; cultivating plants and animals; and tapping into the gentle flow of the seasons and the elements. Mother Nature was key to their survival. A partner in life and love, it became a place to retreat and find inner peace, and still is.

A walk in the woods is a step back in time to when ancient forests carpeted the landscape and wildflowers bloomed in abundance. It allows a glimpse into another world, and helps you reconnect with your roots, both physical and ancestral. The same can be said for any time spent immersed in nature. Whether you are relaxing in the garden, taking a stroll in your local park, or going for a ramble among the fields and meadows, the experience ultimately strengthens your bond with the environment, and boosts wellbeing. The plants and flowers which combine to create each of these colorful vistas are an essential part of this experience, and of your story as a human. They have their own characteristics and tales to tell, which enhance your connection to the natural kingdom.

## WHY FLOWERS?

Admired for their looks and harnessed for a variety of properties, flowers contribute much to the ecosphere, but there's more to these floral beauties than meets the eye. Think about the blooms that you love and how they make you feel. Picture your favorite and recreate it in your mind. While the vision may remind you of the flower, it does not capture every aspect. For you to have the full picture, you need to feel its presence and share the air it breathes, and to know it's back story. Knowing what the flower signifies and the role it has played in the history of the world—your history—will help you understand more about yourself.

By learning about the flower's folklore you will be able to tap into, and harness, its energy. There is much to enjoy in the shape and form of each flower and its distinctive traits. But knowing the myths and legends, the superstitions, and ideas born from them, only adds to the magic and serves to make it real.

## THE NARRATIVES AND HOW TO USE THEM

The stories within this book are based upon myths and legends associated with each bloom from around the world. From fascinating folklore to quirky superstitions, every tale has something magical to contribute, and offers some kind of healing or lesson that can be gleaned from the narrative. You will discover the deeper meaning of each flower, and its distinct symbolism. You will learn how to connect with the bloom and tune in to its unique energy through a simple ritual, and you will form a clearer understanding of what the flower represents, and its importance throughout history.

Some stories feature great love affairs with tragic endings—epic tales of romance and betrayal—while others focus on the simple things in life, such as the day-to-day challenges and the twists and turns of fate, the kindness of strangers, and the wonder of the natural world. While the stories come from all corners of the globe, you will notice that certain areas of folklore are more prominent, for example, the Ancient Greeks had a passion for all things botanical and laid claim to floral myths, choosing to name many of the flowers we know and love today. Further afield in Europe, flowers were the subject of superstition and tradition, and steeped in enchantment.

Organized by when they come into bloom, every story has its place, and you too will settle upon your favorites. Whether you choose to read about those you love the most first, to dip in and out of the pages, or to start at the beginning and work your way through, is up to you. Treat this book as an exercise in foraging. Go with your instincts, and what catches your eye. Let yourself be drawn in by the color and vibrancy of each image, then allow the tale to unfold before your eyes. Use the rituals as a springboard to learn more about the flower and, should you feel inclined, bring it into your world, whether that's through cultivation or an appreciation of it in the wild. Let the beauty inspire you, and drink deep of each bloom's gifts, for they are a reminder of nature's glory, and of the wonder that lives within you.

# Chapter 1
# SPRING

## SPRING ARRIVALS

The skin of the earth trembles in anticipation as the first rays of spring sunshine filter through the trees. This gentle light is what the landscape craves, for it is ready to give birth to all manner of floral delights. From pretty tubular blooms like Tulips, with their cup shaped petals and rainbow shades, to the deep, alluring hues of the Rhododendron, a flower that needs no introduction, or partner to dull it's shine. The blooms within this section are a welcome sight, and their stories are littered with treasures, just as the spring brings its own bounty of pleasure. There is no need to rush when you are in their company, for these flowers like to take their time, to wait until exactly the right moment, and then to emerge, unleashing their radiance for all the world to see and delivering their tale in their own unique style.

# ANENOME
## *Anenome coronaria*

Anenomes come in a range of
colors with small round petals, and
long slender stems.

**FLOWER MEANING** Associated
with forsaken or forgotten love, and
anticipation.

**FOLKLORE ORIGIN** Greece

## APHRODITE AND ADONIS

They say you come into the world as you go out, and
while most births are arduous and hard won, for
Adonis his arrival was even more significant. Born
from the Myrrh tree, that had once been his mother,
he lay dormant within the belly of the trunk until a
swarthy young boar with mighty tusks sliced a hole
into the bark, and out he fell. A tiny babe, plump from
the sap that had sustained his life, it's no wonder he
was such a pretty infant. Even so, his looks would
not protect him from the wrath of the forest or the
creatures of the night. Adonis would not have lasted
till dawn, had it not been for the intervention of the
goddess of love, who happened to be walking by
when he made his entrance.

She lifted him into her arms, and there for a
moment he lay, safe beneath her loving gaze. Of
course, Aphrodite was not known for her motherly
instincts, and although she was smitten by the

infant's charm, her role in the Greek pantheon meant that she had more heavenly concerns, and so she placed the child under the care of Persephone, a young maiden goddess who would have the time and patience to nurture him.

And that could have been the end of the story. But Adonis was more than just mortal. Yes, he was flesh and blood and bones and sinew, governed by ego and the other virtues of man, but there was something otherworldly about his smile, about the way he held himself—a magnetic force that grew with each passing year.

Over time, the child became a man, and the man became a legend, known for his hunting prowess as much as his arrogance. He was not oblivious to his appearance, catching sight of his chiseled features in the rivers and streams.

He would smile and say, "How fine I am! The best hunter in the land, and the best at most things, be it not for the gods!"

Women and deities swooned at the mention of his name, and Adonis adored their attentions. But there was one who loved him more than most. She had seen him transform—the leanness of youth replaced by solid muscle, a strong mind, and an aptitude for the bow. She had watched it all, from her seat on Mount Olympus, and she had smiled, because nothing would stop her now from declaring her true feelings.

The goddess Aphrodite believed that Adonis belonged solely to her, and despite Persephone's pleas to release him, Aphrodite would not comply. And so she won his heart. It was that easy. After all, if she could not capture his ardour, then who could? Being human, he was powerless to fight her advances.

For a time, the couple lived in harmony. Aphrodite in the first flush of love was a pleasure to behold and together they were truly delightful. She the rescuer, he the young babe she had brought into the world now grown into a beautiful man. He complemented her daily, brought her the softest animal skins from his endeavors, and gifted her with the exotic blooms he discovered on his travels. She cosseted his ego, encouraged him in all things, and addressed his every need. It was a marriage made in heaven, and it might have lasted, but then she had the dream.

It plagued the goddess in her sleep with tortuous images of Adonis caught in the throes of the action, on the biggest hunt of his life. One minute astride the beast, the next torn almost in two, his pale face disintegrated before her eyes, the blood spilling in every direction. The sight of it made her scream in terror, waking her from slumber, and shaking their marital bed.

"It was just a dream," he whispered, as he smoothed her brow. But the goddess was not convinced.

"It was a premonition, my love, and one you should listen to."

"I do not believe in such things. I am the best hunter in the land, you have said so yourself. Don't you trust me?

"Yes," she said, "but I trust this vision too. Don't go on the hunt."

Adonis scoffed. "You would have me stay at home, because of some silly dream?" He laughed, and shook his dark curls. "I am going on the hunt, and it will be the biggest and best of my life."

The next day he departed, full of confidence in his own abilities. He strode out with his men, ready to catch the prize boar, the silver backed one said to haunt the woods, and for a while the mood was good. They caught many deer, some hares, and an array of birds, but still the boar eluded him. Adonis was about to admit defeat when he heard a rustle behind him. Before he could turn the creature was upon him, mighty tusks slicing through his flesh. He cried out, and in his anguish locked eyes with his attacker, and in that moment he recognized the beast to be the one who had birthed him from the tree.

As the light went out, and his gazed darkened, Aphrodite flew to his side. She cradled him in her arms, as she had done all of those years ago. All of the grief and sadness poured out of her, and as she shed her last tear the droplets mingled with the blood of Adonis, to create the most beautiful flower she had ever seen.

With delicate round petals and a slender stem, it poked from the earth, and slowly more clusters began to form. The pretty blooms spread at her feet and grew in abundance over the years. Known as Anenomes, they became a symbol of a love forsaken by pride and lost.

## RITUAL TO NURTURE A FLEXIBLE ATTITUDE

These beautiful blooms are associated with the wind and the coming of spring. With this in mind, they represent transition and stepping from one cycle to another.

*You will need: A bunch of Anenomes, a vase of water, and a white candle.*

- Place the Anenomes in a vase of water.
- Light a white candle and position this in front of the vase.
- Sit and gaze into the flame. Notice how it flickers and twists in the air. Let the flame soothe your mind.
- When you're ready, close your eyes and as you inhale, picture an Anemone sprouting from the ground.
- See the slender stem steadily rising and imagine the tiny bud on top. Watch it unfurl to reveal the flowerhead. See the petals dance in the breeze.
- Say, "Like the Anenome, I bend and weave. I embrace the winds of change in my life."

# RHODODENDRON

*Rhododendron*

Rhododendron is a flowering shrub, which can be evergreen or deciduous. It has oval green leaves and produces clusters of flowers that are tubular, bell-shaped, and come in a variety of bright colors.

**FLOWER MEANING** Associated with beauty, nobility, strength, and marriage.

**FOLKLORE ORIGIN** Nepal

## THE BEAUTY OF THE BLOOM

The forests that sweep through Nepal are vast and leafy. It is easy to lose yourself among the dense vegetation, and to be reminded of a time long ago when plants ruled the world, and formed connections, just as humans do now.

Each tree sought a soul mate, a flowery partner whom they could marry, and grow with in life and love. And so the branches and twigs which were once barren and fruitless became beautiful bloom-filled spaces. Flowers by nature are easy upon the eye, and once a tree had settled upon its choice a partnership was formed—but the bloom known as the Rhododendron received little attention. Hidden within the depths of the forest, concealed by verdant shrubs, she waited for a suitor to come and recognize her worth. As the months progressed, and the last vestige of fall gave way to winter's harsh touch, the bushes became brittle and flimsy, and at last she could be seen and appreciated. But the trees were not impressed.

"What a sorry state!" the Fir tree gasped. "This flower has had its day."

"I agree," said the Aster. "There is nothing here to interest me."

The Juniper was equally disgusted. "Where are the pretty blooms? It is no wonder this flower turns its face to the ground."

Even the Birch, who was known for his manners, could not stand to look at the drooping flowerheads. "I would not choose this flower to be my bride!"

And so the Rhododendron was left alone in her sorrow. Steeped in woe, her tears fell along with her remaining petals. She had been shamed because of the way she looked, and yet it was only a part of the cycle of life, and the shifting seasons. If the trees had listened to reason, they would appreciate that with change comes renewal, and rejuvenation. Her beauty, which was by far the most exquisite among the flowers of the forest, would be restored in the spring. The Rhododendron consoled herself that this was part of the process, and that with time she would return to her full glory, which she did when the earth softened, and the new shoots of grass pushed to the surface.

As the wheel of the year turned, so too did the remaining trees seeking a soul mate. Wandering through the forest, they scoured the undergrowth in search of a bloom to couple up with. It was then that they spotted the Rhododendron in exactly the same place as before, languishing in the shade, only this time she danced before their eyes wearing a deep purple velvety ensemble. Her curves flowed in time with the movement of the earth, weaving a sweet scented spell upon the breeze. Each coiffured petal shimmered in the sunlight—she was truly resplendent.

"What manner of flower is this?" asked the Fir. "She is gorgeous."

"I agree," said the Aster. "She is what I have been searching for, a true beauty."

"She will be mine," laughed the Juniper. "Look at the way she moves, I cannot take my eyes off her."

The Birch spoke loudly, his voice drowning out the others. "No, she belongs to me. I will make her *my* bride."

The trees continued to argue their case, and would have carried on into the evening, had it not been for the Rhododendron, who was tired of their bickering.

"I do not belong to any of you," she said defiantly. "You did not want me when I was not in the first flush of youth, when the icy winds battered my leaves and stole my color. You discarded me, believing that you deserved better."

She paused, looking at each in turn. "I will not marry you."

"But, most beautiful one, you need one of us to grow and flourish," said the Birch in his calmest voice. "It is the only way you will survive."

The Rhododendron opened her petals wide and lifted her pretty face to the sun.

"I survived the entire winter alone, and I will thrive by myself. You would only dull my shine and take me for granted. When the cool winds blow and the snow lays thick on the ground, you will cast me off with little thought. I deserve more than that."

The trees stood in silence, for they knew this to be true. Within their roots there grew a thread of admiration for the resilience of this flower.

"I will stand alone, and be my own tree, if that is what I need to be," she said finally.

Admitting defeat, the trees drooped, their branches scathing the forest floor as they realized the error of their ways. In seeking a flawless flower, they had lost the perfect bloom.

The Rhododendron became a symbol of commitment in love. She was the flower of choice when couples cemented their union, for she represented the loyalty needed to grow together. She understood that marriage is a union of two to create something strong and beautiful— the sap within the veins of the tree and the joy within the heart of the flower. The winds of change may cause the petals to wither, but they can never dull the beauty of the bloom.

## RITUAL FOR SELF-LOVE AND TO TAP INTO YOUR INNATE BEAUTY

Rhododendrons come in many sizes and hues but one commonality is their ability to stand tall and proud, perhaps in the knowledge of their own beauty. You can do the same with this ritual for self-love.

*You will need: Some time to reflect, a selection of pictures of Rhododendrons, a journal and a pen.*

- Spread the pictures before you and cast your eye over them. Notice the ones that stand out and ask yourself why.
- Now look at all the blooms and find one thing you like about each.
- Consider how, as humans, we are also alike, and yet distinctly different. We all have qualities and features that make us unique.
- In the journal, make a list of the qualities that you appreciate in yourself.
- Pay attention to the things you like about yourself, and every time you notice something new, add it to your list.
- Use this as a written reminder of your unique beauty.

# TULIP

## *Tulipa*

Tulips have thick green leaves at the base of their stem, and a long stalk. Their flowers are single or double and come in a range of colors.

**FLOWER MEANING** Associated with true love, perfection, and innocence.

**FOLKLORE ORIGIN** Persia

## THE PRINCESS AND THE PEASANT

It was said that Princess Shirin was the jewel in the eye of Persia: a beauty with a golden heart and a smile that could summon the sun. The melody of her laughter was like a delicate waterfall, and when she spoke it was gentle like birdsong, but most impressive of all was her demeanor, for she had a way of making people feel special. As such she was quite the catch, a fact her father the Shah knew too well. Being high born meant that only a prince would do for his precious girl, but try as he might she showed little interest in falling in love. Many princes came to woo her, but they were unsuccessful. The truth was, the princess was already smitten by a local young man, a stonecutter named Farhad.

It had been a chance encounter the day they had met, for the princess loved to disguise her appearance and go walking though the market. She would draw a veil over her pretty face, and don the robes of a serving girl. Within this guise she felt free.

She was able to be with her people, to rub shoulders with the poor and hardworking, and to offer a smile or a word of encouragement to the ailing. This was where she felt at home, and it was on one of her casual walks that their eyes had met, and the arrow of love had struck.

Farhad was completely besotted with the princess, even before he realized who she was. He would do anything to win her hand in marriage, and it was this desire that propelled him to approach the Shah in person and appeal to his better nature.

"I know I am not worthy of your daughter for I am not a man of means or royal blood, but my heart is true, and it belongs to the princess. Please let me prove my worth. Set me any challenge, and I will fulfil it, if it means we can be married."

The Shah looked on with amusement. He had no intention of giving his daughter away to this lowly fool, despite her pleas. Instead he hatched a plan, and set the young man an impossible task, something that would take him decades to achieve.

"Very well, I will set you a challenge fit for a prince, and if you succeed you may marry my daughter."

He smiled and stroked his beard thoughtfully.

"You are a stonecutter, so this should appeal to you. I would like you to dig a passage through the mountains, a canal of sorts, and it should be six lances wide and three lances deep."

The young man nodded. "I will start straight away!"

The Shah smirked, for he knew in his heart that the boy would never succeed, but what he failed to understand was the passion that fuelled Farhad. The love between the two was pure, and powerful, and it gave him the strength and momentum he needed. It tightened his muscles, and allowed the energy to flow, which in turn fired his determination. With nothing but a spade and his crude tools, Farhad set about the mountain, chipping relentlessly into the rock. Under the raging heat of the burning sun and the starry skies of night, when the winds blew sand into his face and he could hardly see, still he worked, and his efforts were rewarded. He was making significant progress, much faster than anyone had anticipated. The Shah was not pleased.

On hearing the news, his face fell.

"He cannot succeed. I must do something to stop this match."

And so, rubbing his hands together, he came up with a new plan, more sinister than the last. He sent word to Farhad that the princess had fallen ill overnight and died from a mysterious sickness.

The stonecutter was heartbroken. He had no reason to be suspicious of the Shah and believed his words to be true. The pain washed over him, and he wailed long into the night. To think he would never be with his love was overwhelming. He couldn't conceive of a world without her in it, and so in the depths of grief, he flung himself off the tip of the mountain.

Princess Shirin, on hearing that Farhad was dead, immediately fled to the mountainside to see his broken body. She too could not comprehend a world without Farhad. He was her soulmate, and that connection would last for an eternity. It seemed to her that there was only one thing she could do. Taking a silver dagger from her belt, she pressed it to the hilt into her chest, and as the blood flowed from her heart, it mingled with that of her love Farhad.

The scarlet liquid pooled upon the dusty ground, and there, where they lay, a Tulip bloomed. It stood upon a single stem, two leaves at the base. The bell-shaped flower with crimson petals looked like an upturned cup overflowing with emotion. And those who saw it were reminded of the innocence of love, and the perfection that comes when two souls who are destined to be together finally unite.

## RITUAL TO PROMOTE SELF-ESTEEM AND BOOST VITALITY

Tulips come in a range of beautiful colors. It's even possible to grow black oness. They emerge in the spring, making them a symbol of hope and potential. Use their pretty hues to lift your emotions and give you a boost.

*You will need: A selection of different colored Tulips, either arranged in a vase or growing in nature.*

- Look at the selection of Tulips in front of you and admire their shape and color.
- Breathe deeply, relax, and instinctively choose one that you're drawn to. You might want to hold the bloom or simply admire it from afar.
- Think about the color you have chosen. What does it mean to you? If you could think of a feeling or a descriptive word associated with this shade, what would it be? For example, if you have an orange tulip in your sights, you might think the color is revitalizing, or that it makes you feel happy.
- As you continue to breathe deeply, imagine holding the Tulip to your heart, feeling the gorgeous hue seep beneath your skin. Imagine absorbing it and making it a part of you.
- Bring the Tulip to mind whenever you need a boost, and to promote the flow of loving energy.

# RED CLOVER
## *Trifolium pratense*

Red clover is a perennial herb with large downy leaves that feature a white "V" shape. The flowers are red to magenta in hue, and form oval clusters.

**FLOWER MEANING** Associated with prosperity, success, industry, and good luck.

**FOLKLORE ORIGIN** Europe

## THE POWER OF THREE

There was once a lad called Jack, a trusting boy who was easily led. Some might say he was a fool, but what he appeared to lack in brains he more than made up for in kindness. That said, there were those who enjoyed poking fun at him, mostly the older lads, who should have known better. They would taunt him by telling tall tales that only he believed, and then they would laugh at his stupidity behind his back. It was cruel, but Jack being Jack, it didn't really bother him. If it gave them something to smile at then he bore them no malice, such was his sweet nature.

One day the older youths were at a loss for something to do and decided to have some fun at Jack's expense.

"Hey, Jack!" they called, as he made his way up the hill to do his daily chores.

"It's a lovely day for an adventure, don't you think?"

Jack smiled and shrugged. "I guess so."

"Did you know that there's a patch of Red Clover that grows on the other side of the hill at this time of year? Don't you know the stories? Red Clover's the fairy favorite. It's magic!"

Jack stopped in his tracks. "How do you know that?"

The gang leader laughed. "Everyone knows! It's no secret." He smiled then and looped his arm in Jack's conspiratorially.

"I can tell you some stories about it, if you like?"

"Oh yes, please," Jack replied in earnest.

And so the boys began to spin their yarn. They told Jack that the leaves, when plucked fresh from the meadow, would give him "fairy sight" if he held them over his eyes for the rest of the day.

"But how will I see?" Jack asked, and the leader chuckled.

"With fairy sight, of course. The fairies will lead you to where you need to be!" And the other boys had nodded in agreement.

They also told him that he would be blessed with fairy gold, and that the blessings would multiply by a threefold, thanks to the number of leaves that the flower bore.

"It's called the power of three," they said confidently, and Jack's eyes had widened at the thought of all that gold.

"Wow!" he gasped. "I'm going to get me some Red Clover right now."

The boys laughed. "You do that Jack, it will bring you good fortune!"

Then as his back turned, they sniggered to themselves.

"What a fool, he's going to look really stupid walking around with leaves pressed to his eyes all day!"

Jack, being Jack, knew in his heart that they were having fun with him, but he also knew that most superstitions were based on fact. It didn't matter how ridiculous they sounded, there was bound to be a kernel of truth in there somewhere, and he was intrigued. He'd never noticed the Red Clover before and he wanted to get a closer look, so he trudged to the top of the hill and back down the other side to find it.

The flower itself was gorgeous, a deep reddish pink cone that stood out upon the stalk, and leaves that were downy and soft to the touch. He could see why folks thought they were magical. There was definitely an air of enchantment to this bloom. Taking the flower gently in his cupped hands, he picked it lightly from the earth and deposited it in his pocket. Then he plucked the leaves, placing them over his eyes.

The heat of the morning sun was soothing, and the ground beneath seemed to meld to his body, like an earthy mattress. Soon Jack was fast asleep, his eyes shielded by the shady leaves. As his slumber deepened he drifted into dream, except it didn't feel like a dream or anything he could have imagined. He found himself at the edge of the woods, standing by a gnarled old tree stump. A flicker of light caught his eye. It seemed to dance around the exposed roots of what was left of the tree, until it settled behind the twisted Oak, and Jack realized it was a fairy.

Leaning closer, he could see the delicate wings, but before he could say anything to the tiny creature there was a flash of light and the fairy disappeared. In its place sat three small slabs of gold, as thick as Jack's arm. Quickly, he picked them up and put them in his pocket. He couldn't believe his luck and would have jumped for joy, had it not been for the loud clapping noise that distracted him.

"What the. . . ." he mumbled, as several sets of hands hauled him upward. It was the lads from earlier. They surrounded him in a circle.

"Wake up, Jack! You didn't really think that the Red Clover would help you see the fairies, did you?" They sneered and batted the leaves from his sleepy eyes.

"You're such a fool!" the leader scoffed and poked him in the chest. "You'll believe anything anyone tells you. Come on, let's leave this idiot to his daydreaming." Jack watched them go and didn't say a word.

When they were out of earshot, he let his hand slip inside his pocket. He was hoping to pull out the Red Clover from earlier, but instead his fingers alighted upon something cold and smooth, something that felt remarkably like a slab of gold. Carefully he pulled all three pieces free and held them up to the light. It hadn't been a dream, the fairies really had led him to where he needed to be! It was then that he remembered their words from earlier.

"The power of three." Three slabs of gold, meant the wealth was threefold.

Jack being Jack, he didn't boast about his sudden good fortune. He simply smiled, thanked the Red Clover fairy, and continued on his way.

...................................................................................

## RITUAL TO HELP YOU SET INTENTIONS

The four leafed clover has always been considered lucky, but three leaves are equally powerful. Three is a potent number in mythology, which can help you set intentions and focus the mind.

*You will need: Somewhere to sit outside, and a notebook and pen.*

- Take a notepad and a pen and sit somewhere among the flowers.
- Write 1, 2, 3 down the side of the page, and by number 1 write one thing you'd like to achieve this month. Make this something simple and achievable to give you confidence.
- By number 2 write something you'd like to achieve this year, such as, "get a promotion," or "pass an exam."
- By number 3 write down something you'd like to achieve in three years. Pick a goal that is personal to you, such as, "start a business."
- Reflect on all three goals, and starting with the first, think of smaller steps that will help you achieve each one.

# SOLOMON'S SEAL
## *Polygonatum*

Solomon's Seal is a woodland perennial with arching stems and pretty whiteish green bell-shaped flowers. Its leaves are smooth, pleated, and paired along the stem.

**FLOWER MEANING** Associated with wisdom, supernatural power, peace, and good triumphing over evil.

**FOLKLORE ORIGIN** Israel

## SOLOMON'S REST

The world of the supernatural is closer than people think, with the strangest, most exotic creatures on the doorstep. It takes a certain kind of woman (and her cat) to confront such phenomenon and triumph, as Enid was to learn one morning in May.

The seasons were at a crossroads that day, the freshness of spring still colored the landscape, but the meadows were bathed in a golden glow, a hint that summer was imminent. The air was mellow and tinged with warmth and Enid was glad of the gentle heat. It felt like a positive omen for the future, which was just as well for she had moved into a new home, and one with a reputation.

The cottage, known as Solomon's Rest, had been plagued with stories of demons in its history. As far as Enid was concerned it was all stuff and nonsense. She had visited the cottage several times, and it seemed perfectly pleasant and ideal for what she

had in mind. The yard at the back was a haven for wildlife and there was plenty of room for her cultivate a vegetable patch. Rambling roses framed the door and honeysuckle caressed the stone walls, but by far the most abundant flower was the cottage's namesake, Solomon's Seal, which grew in fragrant fluted arches along the path. The delicate creamy flowers looked so graceful as they bobbed in the breeze and Enid felt they were inviting her to stay. And so she moved into the tiny home, with her black cat Methuselah and a heap of books to keep her occupied, and that could have been the end of it. Except that the villagers had been right. Solomon's Rest was not what it seemed. . . . It started that morning with the sound of drumming which seemed to emanate from the fireplace. Not one to suffer fools, Enid checked outside, convinced that it was some of the local youths playing a prank, but there was no one to be seen and no evidence of drums. Then throughout the day as she began to sort through her belongings and position her books, she would hear the sound of laughter and singing too, strained eery notes that seemed to seep through the floorboards.

"Methuselah, investigate!" she ordered the bemused feline, but the cat feigned disinterest and continued to lick his paw.

Enid, not easily deterred, searched every room in the cottage but could find nothing to explain the strange noises.

"I must be imagining it," she thought. Even so a trickle of fear was working its way up her spine. She couldn't deny that the day's events had unsettled her. Perhaps the villagers had been right.

That night she settled down in front of the fire, a book upon her lap, and Methuselah at her feet. The noises of the day had been put to the back of her mind and would have stayed that way, but a sudden gust of wind caused the flames to leap through the grate. A spectral hand lashed at her skirt, and Enid fell backward as the inferno continued to dance out of the fire grate. Gradually a smoky form began to take shape, fusing with the blaze to create a genie shape that rose in wisps from the hearth.

The hideous creature unleashed a roar, causing Enid to scramble further away. The only thing that stood between them was Methuselah, whose arched back and puffed tail seemed to fill the room. The creature wavered, stalled by the cat's ferocity, and eventually receded into the fire, leaving a pile of ash upon the floor.

The tales had been true! There was a supernatural being in her home, but she wasn't about to let it control her life. Enid, being a practical woman, instantly went to her books. There had to be a way to get rid of the fiery monster, and indeed there was, and it was on her doorstep. The creature was a jinn, an underworld demon that had somehow attached itself to her abode. It would, given time, consume her and all who lived there if it grew in strength, but there was a way to stop it escaping the hearth and wreaking havoc. According to legend, the seal of King Solomon's signet ring had the power to control demons and genies, the strange markings held sway over the supernatural realm. While Enid did not have the ring, she did have the flower of the same name which bore the seal's markings upon its roots.

In the morning she picked a handful of the pretty blooms and exposed the roots with their strange indentations. She soaked them in water, to produce a solution that she could use on the Jinn once she'd lit the fire.

The following evening she sat in wait with trusty Methuselah at her side. Together they watched the initial sparks of the fire flicker and then take shape as they had previously. But before the jinn could become solid, Enid stood and dowsed it with the sacred water.

"By the power of King Solomon, and the marks of his seal, you are trapped in this fire. You will never be real. You are mine to command, you must always obey. I will keep you in chains, to the end of my days."

The demon's eyes flared for a second, and then he withered away, swallowed by the crackling fire. The spell had worked. The Solomon's Seal, which she had been so drawn to, had saved her life, and welcomed her to this home. Demon or not, she would remain there, with the help of the pretty bloom, her moggy companion Methuselah, and the ancient covenant of a once great king.

## RITUAL TO PROMOTE NEW GROWTH AND INNER PEACE

Solomon's Seal makes a beautiful addition to any yard. Best planted in the spring, these delicate white flowers have a calming presence. This ritual will help you to harness this peace for yourself.

*You will need: A shaded spot in your yard, compost, a trowel and gardening gloves, Solomon's Seal plants, and a watering can.*

- Find a shady spot in your yard, beneath a tree, or a cluster of other leafy plants, and begin to mark out the position of your plants.
- Ensure the soil is moist by adding in a thin layer of compost.
- Press lightly with your hands, wearing gardening gloves. Breathe deeply and make every action count, as you prepare the earth.
- Take your trowel and dig holes that are 4–6 inches (10–15 centimeters) deep.
- Gently position the Solomon's Seal plants, then surround with soil and water well.
- Tend to your plants regularly to nurture new growth.

# DAFFODIL

*Narcissus*

Daffodils are a bulbous perennial with a single long stem bearing a large trumpet-shaped bloom, surrounded by six petal-like tepals. They are usually yellow, but other shades have been cultivated.

**FLOWER MEANING** Associated with rebirth, transformation and new beginnings, and spring.

**FOLKLORE ORIGIN** Greece

## THE LAST WORDS

A long time ago in ancient Greece there lived a boy called Narcissus. A beautiful child by all accounts, his skin was milky soft and smooth, and his wide eyes sparkled like the sun-kissed ocean. His smile could light up a room, and his cheeks were rosy red apples. Silky golden curls framed his face and accentuated the gentle features.

His mother, recognizing that he was special, took him to an oracle who professed that the boy was indeed gifted by the gods.

"His stunning beauty will take him far, as long as he never sees his own reflection. Be sure to remove all of the mirrors from your home, and in return he will live a long and happy life."

Being a dutiful woman she took the words to heart and banished every single mirror within the vicinity, and just as the oracle had said, the boy grew into a handsome and successful young man.

31

As expected, he had many admirers, but it was the sweet nymph Echo who fell wholeheartedly for his charms. She hadn't had the best start in life, having been enlisted by the god Zeus to cover up his infidelities by distracting his wife Hera. As the older woman tried in vain to uncover her husband's betrayals, Echo kept her occupied, twittering away like a song bird about every subject under the sun. The goddess became wise to Zeus's plan and was annoyed at the nymph for her part in the deception, so she cursed her.

"May your loose tongue be silenced. You will never speak freely again, my dear. You will only be able to repeat the last words that are said to you, and that is all."

The nymph did not fully understand the hex that had been placed upon her. It was only when she encountered another of her kind, that the truth was revealed when they asked, "Echo, what befalls you on this lovely day?"

And she could only reply, *"Day, day, day. . . ."*

Distraught at the reality of her situation, Echo fled deep into the woods, and it was on her way that she crossed paths with Narcissus. The sight of him stopped her in her tracks. The sun shone from within him and warmed her heart. She reached out to touch him, but he flinched and turned away.

"Leave me alone," he snapped.

And all poor Echo could say in return was, *"Alone, alone, alone. . . ."*

He looked at her with disgust in his eyes. "What are you? A freak?"

*"Freak, freak, freak . . . "* she replied.

She tried again to get close to him, her slender fingers brushed his cheek, but he recoiled, his face twisting with repulsion.

"Do not touch me, you are not worthy!"

*"Worthy, worthy, worthy. . ."* she whispered, her eyes full of tears.

Narcissus looked down his nose at her, for she was indeed beneath him, at least in his mind. "I could never love you," he snarled, then turned on his heel and headed deeper into the forest.

Echo crumbled, her tiny form hidden by the undergrowth, as she cried, *"Love you, love you, love you."*

She could not understand how he could be so cruel, and the gods were also angered by his behavior. While they tried not to intervene in an obvious way, it just so happened that Mother Nature would provide them with the perfect punishment.

Narcissus strode through the woody glade oblivious to everything, including the deities' wrath. He pushed past brambles and leaves, charging into the thickest, tallest trees, and there at a small pool he stopped to quench his thirst. Cupping his hands, he scooped up the clear liquid, and it was then that he caught sight of his face for the first time. As he was not accustomed to his own reflection, he assumed what he saw was a water spirit trapped beneath the surface of the stream.

"How beautiful you are!" he exclaimed, and plunged his hands deep into the water, but the image disappeared each time he tried to reach it.

"Do not worry, my love, I will find a way to be with you." He swooned, for he was totally smitten. He believed he was in love with some kind of nymph, and in that moment he pledged his heart.

"I promise, I will never leave you. I love you."

And so he lay by the water's edge, day and night, whispering sweet nothings to his own reflection.

The gods were amused at first. It seemed a fitting price to pay for his conduct with Echo, but after a time they became worried. Narcissus was so enamored with himself that he would not move. He did not eat or drink, he simply gazed at himself, trapped in a trance.

In the end they decided to act, if only to retain the superficial splendor of his face and preserve it for an eternity. They transformed him into a flower, a sunshine yellow bloom called a Daffodil. The wistful petals matched his golden curls, and the fragrant scent captured the essence of his beauty. The nodding bloom grew along the river bank, its pretty face constantly drooped toward the water to catch its reflection; it was a reminder of the shameful narcissism which led to his demise.

The last words he said before he changed completely were, ". . . . love you, love you, love you."

## RITUAL TO PROMOTE THE FLOW OF JOY

Daffodils have a long association with good fortune and happiness. It's a common belief in folklore that filling your home with these spring blooms will promote the flow of positive energy into the home. The color yellow is also associated with joy and enthusiasm.

*You will need: A vase of water, two small bunches of Daffodils, and some yellow ribbon.*

- Fill the vase with fresh water, and pop in one of the bunches.
- Leave the Daffodils in the vase on a window ledge, or close to your front door. Make sure that wherever you position them, you can see them on entering and leaving your home.
- As you see them, smile, and say the affirmation, "Happiness flows into my life," out loud or in your head.
- Take the remaining bunch of Daffodils and tie a yellow bow around the stems, then gift them to a friend or family member.

# HYACINTH
## *Hyacinthus orientalis*

Hyacinths have a single thick spike of fragrant star-shaped flowers that come in an array of colors. Their stalk has a small bract of leaves below it.

**FLOWER MEANING** Associated with passion, jealousy, forgiveness, and rebirth.

**FOLKLORE ORIGIN** Greece

## THE HEART OF THE SUN

There once lived a mortal man, more beautiful than any being that had ever walked the earth. Born beneath the shade of a palm tree, upon the Greek isle of Delos, this tiny babe was to become the Prince of Sparta, and his name was Hyacinthus. Destined for greatness, it was only a matter of time before he caught the attention of the gods. Some say his handsome face was his fortune, but others admit that his beauty was also his downfall. When people saw him they would swoon, and swear that they had been blessed, for the power of his gaze was such that their hearts would instantly melt.

As expected, he had many lovers. Most prominent was his affair with Thamyris, the son of Philammon, which caused heads to turn and sparked jealousy among his peers. But there were otherworldly beings who were also concerned with his love life,

in particular the sun god Apollo, who it is said shone brighter at the mention of his name.

Apollo was never one to wait for attention, and once he'd set his mind upon a love tryst, there was no denying his affections, so while Hyacinthus languished in the arms of Thamyris, it was destined to be short-lived. His lover challenged the Muses to a contest, a trial that was fated from the start with the intervention of the green-eyed god Apollo who influenced proceedings. Unsurprisingly Thamyris lost and was destroyed in the process, leaving Hycanthus free to be wooed by another.

Bathing him in a light more radiant than any heavenly being, Apollo's rays soothed the prince's grieving soul, and soon they were ensconced in a passionate affair that would take them all over the world. The god was truly smitten and wanted to share his life with the handsome mortal. Flying through the skies in Apollo's golden chariot pulled by swans, Hyacinthus was full of joy. He had never in his wildest dreams expected any of this and wanted to spend every minute with his new beau. The feeling was mutual, and Apollo was happy to teach his companion new skills, so that he would be even more accomplished in his daily life.

First he taught Hyacinthus how to play the lyre, so that they could make sweet music together. Then he showed him how to hunt using a bow, so that the prince would never be without sustenance, and could show off his talents to his noble friends. Once he had perfected this skill, Apollo decided it was time to teach him how to throw the discus. This would be the pinnacle of his achievements and give him the edge against any competitor.

A keen student, Hyacinthus watched as Apollo gave him a practical demonstration. With all of his godly strength, he threw the discus into the air. Higher and higher it flew, and with such force, that it split the clouds in two. Hyacinthus gasped. He had never seen such might and wanted to prove himself worthy in Apollo's presence, and so he ran as fast as he could to retrieve the giant discus. It soared through the heavens, eventually returning to earth with such ferocity that it hit the young prince on the back of his skull, slicing it open. The blow struck hard, and he fell to his knees. As the blood flowed freely, he took his last breath.

Apollo was devastated, scooping up the broken body of his true love as he tried in vain to save him, and while he was blessed with healing power, it was not enough to bring Hyacinthus back from the dead.

Heartbroken, the god slowly began to rise to his feet. There was nothing to be done here, except to mourn his loss, but as he stood and glanced back at the ground where his lover lay, he noticed scarlet flecks of blood which had sprayed from the head wound onto the earth. The sparkling gems made the dusty soil shimmer under the light of the god's sun, and slowly, steadily, they began to transform into beautiful, jeweled blooms.

Apollo smiled. It seemed fitting that his love should be reborn into a new form, and one that would show off his beauty. And so the Hyacinth flower came into being—a many petaled plume of the most vibrant hues upon a tall sturdy stalk. It grew voraciously, in clumps of flowers upon the mound where the prince had fallen. Not only that but his people, in honor of Hyacinthus, decided to mark his passing with a festival which lasted three days. In that time they celebrated his life and commemorated his death. They honored the winter months as a time to withdraw and to go within, just as their prince had gone to his final resting place. And they rejoiced upon his return as a beautiful flower in the summer months. They called this festival Hyacinthia, and it became a yearly occurrence, and way to remember the mortal who had stolen the heart of the sun.

## RITUAL TO REVITALIZE AND HARNESS YOUR NATURAL BEAUTY

Hyacinth bulbs are toxic, but the leaves and flowers are used in many preparations for the skin. Being anti-microbial and anti-fungal, the leaf extract is used to treat eczema. The flower is one of the first to appear during the spring, and a symbol of rebirth.

*You will need: Somewhere comfortable to sit, and a picture of a Hyacinth or the real thing to gaze at.*

- To begin, spend a few minutes looking at the Hyacinth. Notice its size, shape, and structure, and the poise with which it holds itself.
- Notice the strength of the stalk and the way the bloom points up to the heavens, while being grown from a bulb deep in the soil.
- Close your eyes and imagine that you are like the Hyacinth. Feel your connection with the earth and how it supports you, as you sit.
- Imagine your body is the stalk, strong and true as it points upward. Take a deep breath in and as you exhale, lengthen your spine, and feel the gentle stretch.
- Now turn your attention to the flower and picture a beautiful bloom sprouting from the center of your scalp. Imagine each petal opening and becoming more vibrant with every breath.
- Feel the joy as you are reborn in flower form and unleash your natural beauty.

# BLUEBELL
## *Hyacinthoides non-scripta*

Bluebell flowers hang from one side of a drooping stem. Their flowers are thin tubular bells, and usually violet blue in hue.

**FLOWER MEANING** Associated with humility, virtue, gratitude, and magic.

**FOLKLORE ORIGIN** Scotland

## THE OLD MAN'S BELLS

As early as the 1600s it was common knowledge among those who gathered flowers that Bluebells were inherently magical. A herald of spring, these pretty bell-shaped blooms would carpet the most ancient of woodland, spreading into the darkest corners of the forest where the shadows fell. In between exposed tree roots they would cluster, gathering in mossy knolls and bathing the ground in the sweetest blue haze. And while most would agree it was a glorious sight and much welcomed after the harsh winter months, there were some who would avoid the woods at this time, believing in the darker folklore that surrounded this pretty flower.

Deborah was not one of these, she cared little for tradition or the beliefs of others and liked to make up her own stories. It wasn't that she was cruel, at least not at first. Those that knew her would say she was lots of fun to be around. A prankster, with a penchant for tall tales, Deborah liked to tell lies. Over the years she had perfected the art, starting with the smaller white lies that everyone has told, such as, "Oh yes, you look so pretty in that dress!" when really she thought the opposite, or, "I can't do my chores today, my belly hurts," when in fact she was perfectly fine. Deborah could feign illness, pleasure, anger, and fear at the drop of a hat, and would have been most at home upon the stage.

As she grew, she became adept at pulling the wool over the eyes of others, and her lies became more elaborate, to the point that they would cause trouble. In particular, she liked to create havoc when it came to romance, especially with her friends and acquaintances. She would spread rumors of one liking another that were untrue, and then watch as each fell over themselves to either avoid the other person, or respond to the alleged interest, which usually led to a broken friendship. In some cases it went further, and genuine warmth turned to hate as Deborah watched with amusement. Soon everyone was aware of her ability to deceive and grew wary.

"She must be stopped, before she does real damage!" her friends agreed. "But how? We can't stop her telling tales."

"There is one thing that might help," said one of the quieter of the bunch. "I have heard that Bluebells work wonders for such an affliction. Worn as a necklace it renders the wearer unable to tell a lie."

"But isn't that Old Man's magic?"

"Yes, it's dark sorcery, but if it works it's worth it."

The friends decided that this was the only course of action, and so that day they went Bluebell picking. Later they presented Deborah with the necklace, a delicate chain looped together by the stems that hung loosely around her neck. The bells fluttered in the wind.

Deborah was surprised by the gift. She had not expected something so lovely, and even felt a pang of guilt at some of the mischief she had created, but soon shrugged it off. After all, telling tales was what she did best, and it gave her so much pleasure to watch the drama unfold. But that was about to change, for the necklace worked like a charm.

Every time Deborah opened her mouth to spin one of her stories or tell a lie, it seemed the words got choked in her throat, and she couldn't speak at all. She tried everything, approaching her deceit by rephrasing things, and even singing to herself, but the lies just would not come while she was wearing the necklace. At night however, when she removed it before bed, she was able to think straight, and the words flowed easily if she said them out loud. Deborah had always been blessed with brains, and swiftly realized that the Bluebell chain was a charm to stop her wayward tongue.

"How dare they curse me!" she spat. "I will have them for this! I will get my revenge, but first I must rid myself of this hex."

The following day Deborah made her way to the woods, where the

Bluebells grew in abundance. Trampling on the carpet at her feet, she ripped the necklace to shreds, tearing the petals of the fragile flowers into tiny pieces and scattering them into the wind.

"I am free of this curse!" she cried.

But while she had broken the lie charm, she had incurred the wrath of another, much darker force—Old Man with his horned brow and cloven feet. The keeper of the bells, if tales were to be believed.

In retaliation the Bluebells beneath her feet began to bristle and then chime—a dull throbbing sound that filled her head. Their blooms swayed in the breeze, their bells humming low. The ground began to rumble, and Deborah lost her footing. She fell into a particularly dense patch of the flowers, but instead of the soft landing she'd expected, gnarly rootlike fingers grasped at her, pulling her deeper into the damp soil. Hands that were weathered by time and blistered by the fires of hell tore at her dress, and dragged her deeper underground, and though she yelled, her screams were muffled by the blanket of blue above her.

It soon became known among the townsfolk that Deborah had vanished, although no one knew how or why she had disappeared so abruptly. To this day, some say they still hear her, but only at the onset of spring if you walk among the first Bluebells and listen carefully. Then you might catch a whisper of her lies.

## RITUAL TO PROMOTE A SENSE OF WONDER AND FOR INSPIRATION

Bluebells are commonly found in woodlands during the spring. They're an uplifting sight, and the perfect flower to reconnect you with nature.

*You will need: Some time in the woods, a journal, and a pen.*

- Find a patch of woodland and go on a Bluebell hunt. Take your time as you meander through the trees and engage all of your senses.
- Listen to the crunch of the woody undergrowth beneath your feet, hear the sounds of the leaves and birds fluttering in the branches.
- Breathe in the earthy aroma at the heart of the woods, taste it upon your tongue and let it fill your lungs.
- Gaze up at the tree canopy, and down at your feet. If you're lucky enough to find a patch of Bluebells, take some time to admire them.
- Use your journal to make a note of how you feel, and what you have gained from this experience.
- If you feel inspired, have a go at drawing a Bluebell, or writing a short poem to capture its beauty.

# PEONY

*Paeonia lactiflora*

Peonies have big showy flowers that consist of single, double, or semi-double layers of petals that come in a range of vibrant colors. Their leaves are large and glossy.

**FLOWER MEANING** Associated with honor, respect, wealth, and nobility.

**FOLKLORE ORIGIN** China

## THE KING OF FLOWERS

If you visit Luoyang in the month of April, you will be greeted by a parade of Peonies. These exquisite wide-petaled blooms boast an array of colors fit for an imperial dynasty. Known as the "King of Flowers" the Peony symbolizes nobility, and generates respect and honor in equal measure, for when it blossoms it tells a story of nature's will: something more powerful than human or deity.

Once upon a time, during the Tang dynasty, when the capital city Chang'an was the seat of the Imperial family, there lived an empress named Wu Zetian. She was a wilful and spontaneous woman who enjoyed the luxury that her position within this ancient dynasty had gifted her. When she clicked her fingers, it seemed that even the elements would respond to her demands. The breeze would ruffle her skirts, the sun would shine a little brighter, and the birds would puff out their chests and sing their sweetest melodies. Empress Wu knew how to command respect and get exactly what she wanted, when she wanted it.

One day, during a mild winter, the empress decided to take a ceremonial tea in the royal flower yard. She arrived with a small entourage and settled upon a cushioned plinth beneath her favorite cherry tree. But all was not as she expected, for there were no flowers in bloom except for the sweet Jasmine, which clung desperately to the promise of the coming spring.

The lacklustre vista made her heart sink, and a wave of melancholy washed over her. "Where are my beautiful blooms?" she cried.

Her personal maid shuffled closer and with a head bowed whispered, "Most honorable one, it is still winter, the flowers will not show their faces till spring."

The empress sighed. "How depressing! I need color and beauty to lift my senses." She paused for a moment and then clicked her fingers. "Bring me paper and something to write with, I will enlist the help of the flower goddess by writing her a poem."

Quickly the maid returned with a sheet of paper and a quill and placed it carefully at her feet. The empress wasting little time began to compose a rhyme that would appeal to the flower goddess.

"Let it be spring, let my heart sing. As if it were May, upon this day. Let the flowers appear, tomorrow, right here." Sealing the ditty, she gave it to the maid to leave as an offering at the holy temple, then continued to sip her tea, safe in the knowledge that her wishes would be fulfilled.

The following morning the empress made her way to the flower yard. As she walked through the golden arch, a wall of color filled her field of vision. It seemed as if every flower in the yard had come to life overnight. A profusion of candy pink blossom spilled forth from the trees, huge exotic blood red blooms with orange-tipped petals billowed from giant bushes, and all was abundant and fresh. The soothing buzz of bees filled her ears. She could sense their industry, and this pleased her greatly. She breathed deeply and inhaled the honeyed aroma; the scent of new growth filled her with hope, and yet something wasn't quite right. She paused, glanced to the left and right. Yes, there was something missing, something she needed to make this picture complete.

"My Peonies!" she exclaimed. "Why do they not bloom?"

She spun around, looking for any sign of her favorite flowers. She walked briskly the length and breadth of the path, examining the earth.

"I do not understand, why do they not obey me?"

"Most honorable one, perhaps you should seek the help of the goddess again?" suggested the maid.

Empress Wu was not impressed, but decided this was the best course of action. Once more she petitioned the deity to assist, this time offering prayers and incense as a way of encouraging her, and while the flower goddess did her best, even she could not rouse the sleeping bloom.

It didn't matter how many times the empress clicked her fingers, or who she enlisted to help, nothing worked. The Peonies were stubborn and would not budge from their cosy flower beds.

In a fit of anger the empress banished the flower in its entirety from the capital city. "If it doesn't wish to bloom for me, then it shall not bloom at all!" she yelled. "Send it to Luoyang where it can languish in shame."

And so all of the royal Peonies were uprooted, and taken to Luoyang, and while they could have withered and died during the journey, or not bothered to blossom upon arrival, the strangest thing happened once they passed through the city gates. It was as if the Peonies had been touched by heavenly magic. One by one they unfurled, in a graceful dance which revealed their dazzling beauty. It was a breathtaking sight and fit for an empress, although she wasn't there to witness the miracle.

From that day forward, the beautiful Peony would command respect from those who cared to grow it, whether in Asia, Europe, or anywhere else in the world. Never one to blossom outside of its season, this noble flower cannot be rushed, but is always worth the wait.

## RITUAL TO CALM AN ANXIOUS, RESTLESS MIND

Historically, Peonies were a popular choice to heal gout, arthritis, and chest infections. Thought to improve irritability and restlessness, Peony petals can be eaten raw or steamed.

*You will need: Somewhere quiet to sit and relax, and a Peony flower any color of your choice.*

- Make sure you are comfortable and that you have a good view of the flower, whether it's in bloom in your yard, or in a vase.
- Relax and spend a few minutes gazing at the bloom. Engage all of your senses as you take in its beauty. Notice the size and shape of the flowerhead, any delicate patterns among the petals, the richness of the color, and how it makes you feel when you look at it.
- Imagine what it would be like to touch the flower, to hold it in your hands. What would it feel like?
- Breathe deeply and inhale any aroma, whether real or imagined.
- Now close your eyes and take a couple of minutes to recreate the image of the Peony. Bring to mind all of the little details that you noticed when you were gazing at it.
- Enjoy the picture you have created, and then open your eyes and compare it with the real thing.
- This mindful exercise helps you engage with the present moment by concentrating solely on the beauty of the Peony.

# COWSLIP
## *Primula veris*

Cowslip is a herbaceous perennial
with rounded leaves. Its nodding
yellow blooms grow in clusters upon
long stalks.

**FLOWER MEANING** Associated
with grace, faith, adventure,
and beauty.

**FOLKLORE ORIGIN** Europe

### THE KEYS OF HEAVEN

Every creature, human or otherwise, has the potential
for greatness, but while many live up to such aspira-
tions, there are some who believe they are not worthy.
For these people, even the thought of such eminence
is beyond them. It is not because they lack the talent
or tenacity required to achieve their heart's desires, it
is simply because they have never been encouraged
and do not realize that the Keys of Heaven are within
their grasp.

The universal power that some might call God,
and others the guiding hand of fate, has always
been aware of this failing. After all, God created all
things, and that includes humankind. He knows that
the creatures of the earth sometimes need a loving
push. From the birds in the trees, who might have
languished upon the branches had it not been for
the zealous winds that whipped at their wings, to the
bees nestling in their hives, but needing the nectar to

feed their family, it seems that every being requires some reminder that they can achieve anything.

And so it was with Peter, named after the apostle by his church loving family. A strapping young lad, who by rights should have been full of energy and verve for a life working the land. It seemed that Peter wanted to spend his days lazing in the sunshine, and doing nothing to help his nearest and dearest or the community that he was a part of.

Peter had no interest in his father's farm work, but it wasn't because he didn't care. He simply didn't believe that he had the skill or wits to do anything of service. He believed he was useless at all things, and as such it was better that he did nothing. His parents struggled to cope with their wayward son, and instead of encouraging him, had spent most of his life telling him what a failure he was. The constant chastising had taken its toll and Peter now believed he was worthless, and so when the cows that belonged to his father went missing, Peter did little to help.

"You're no son of mine," his father muttered bitterly, "twiddling your thumbs, when you could be out looking for my cows."

"But what use would I be?" Peter reasoned. "You have said yourself I am not worth bothering with. I am not a farmer like you."

Peter's father growled, "Enough of your lip, lad! If you're not going to help, get out of my sight!"

Peter was happy to oblige. He knew what his father's moods were like, and he didn't wish to be anywhere near him. Instead he ambled through the meadows, over the fields laden with crops, and on toward the next valley, wishing he could keep walking forever and leave his life behind. Nobody would miss him, and he wouldn't miss being there, or anywhere for that matter.

"What's the point . . ." he sobbed. "I *am* useless, there is no reason for me at all."

It was then that the clouds that had gathered above his head seemed to split in two, and out of the gray, a voice spoke into Peter's heart.

"My boy, there is greatness in you, just as there was in your namesake, never forget that."

The voice made the earth tremble, and Peter shivered in fear.

"Please, please leave me alone, I have done nothing!" he cried.

"That is true, but it is time for that to change. You have the power to be anything you want. You just need to believe in yourself."

Peter paused. "But how? I am useless."

"No you are not. Behold, the Keys of Heaven await you."

Peter looked around and in the stillness of the moment, when it seemed that even the air ceased to move, and the carpet of grass at his feet began to bristle. Tiny filaments of bright green were bursting between the darker blades of grass, curling and unfurling before his eyes, to reveal a meadow of golden blooms. They sprang to life instantly, with yellow lobes and distinctive orange spots, each of the fluted flowers framed by a rosette of leaves.

"The Keys of Heaven . . ." Peter whispered, "I have never seen such beauty." And neither had the cows, for they were drawn to this pretty display. They appeared from over the horizon, moving at first slowly, then faster until they reached where he stood. Huddling together, they grazed among the flora, and Peter recognized them straight away for they were his father's herd.

"Thank you for this gift," he said, turning his face upward, and for the first time in his life, he prayed. His words were imbued with gratitude, and it was then that he learned about the flower spread at his feet. When Saint Peter had scattered the Keys of Heaven upon the earth, wherever they fell Cowslips grew in abundance.

When he returned home with his father's cows, Peter finally had a purpose, and a role to aspire to. He knew in his heart what he wanted to do with his life, and how he wanted to serve the god who had encouraged him. While he would never follow in his father's footsteps as a farmer, his path was clear, and it led to the church. He had the Keys of Heaven within his grasp, and he finally believed in himself, thanks to a higher power and the Cowslips in the meadow.

## RITUAL TO LIFT THE SPIRITS AND PROMOTE A SENSE OF ADVENTURE

Cowslips were originally called "Cow Slop" because they had a habit of springing up in between the cow dung. The name has been distorted over time by accent and pronunciation. They're a glorious sight when in full bloom, and walking among them can instantly lift your mood.

*You will need: Somewhere to walk through fields and meadows, and your phone or a camera.*

- You're going to take a wildflower walk through the countryside. If you can, map out a route in advance which takes you through fields and meadows, where you're likely to see Cowslips growing.
- This is a mindful walk, so every couple of minutes stop and engage each of your senses.
- Consider what you can see, hear, smell, taste, touch, and feel. Run through each sense and make a note of anything that stands out.
- Take this opportunity to look at the wildflowers that carpet your path, and take pictures of those that appeal, to identify them later.
- Be sure to look for Cowslips, or if you find an area where cows are grazing, or have grazed, take a closer look to see if you can spot any.

# COLUMBINE
*Aquilegia vulgaris*

Columbine is a tall herbaceous perennial with distinctive five-petaled flowers, and backward-learning spurs. The leaves are a dull green and made up of three rounded leaflets.

**FLOWER MEANING** Associated with love, fertility, fortitude, and courage.

**FOLKLORE ORIGIN** Scandinavia

## FREYA'S FANCY

Across the ocean, where the gray clouds hover and the land is carved from stone, where plateaus stretch as far as the eye can see and icy mountains command the view, that is where you will find this beauty. Thriving in the wetlands, and at the highest of altitudes, it weaves among the stars and the gods, for it is Freya's fancy, her bloom of choice. A flower of great standing among the Norse people, and a symbol of courage, allure, and love. After all love is the goddess Freya's currency and her motivation in all things. Always prepared for battle, she fights for the love of her people and chooses which warriors will frequent the halls of Valhalla, with her heart.

And like all deities at that time, she had her symbols: the cloak of hawk feathers which allowed the wearer to fly; the Brisingamen necklace, forged by the dwarves after she spent many nights in their company; and her beautiful chariot, drawn by two enormous blue cats, a gift from the god Thor.

It was no surprise that men and gods would present such treasures to her, for she was the most beautiful woman in all of the kingdoms. It was said that once you had gazed into her deep blue eyes, you would be unable to refuse her anything—a truth that she used to her advantage. And so life was good for the goddess. She only had to smile and flutter her eyelashes to get what she wanted, but there was one thing that eluded her. Something that every goddess needs—a flower.

Freya sought a bloom which could represent everything she stood for, and that was the problem, for she was not simply a goddess of love. Like any woman, she was a complex creature with many facets to her personality. While she could be incredibly romantic, and kindhearted, she was known for her passionate encounters and lusty appetites. A being of great beauty, she would scrub up for battle wearing her armor and wielding a sword better than any man. She was aggressive, calculating, courageous in spirit, and imbued with a need for action, and a thirst for blood. Never one to back down from a fight, Freya's confidence was evident in every undertaking. To be fair, the Vikings were more than a little in awe of her. She was not one to suffer fools or those with an inflated ego and knew how to put anyone in their place. And so finding a flower that could capture every part of her seemed an impossible task.

There were those who thought a Rose might be the ideal choice. A flower of incomparable beauty, and a symbol of love, it was surely the perfect match for Freya who encompassed love in its many forms. But while she liked the look of the bloom and its significance, it did not fit with her lust for life, or her feisty ways. When she held it in her hands, she felt nothing of the strength that flowed through her veins. Others suggested the Harebell, with its delicate fluted blooms, resilient and pretty, but hardly a fitting icon for the most beautiful woman in the world. Freya needed a flower that was large and showy, a vibrant breathtaking bloom that could command attention. The Alpine Thistle was considered an option. Spiky, strong, and sturdy, surely this would be a match for the goddess, but again what it gained in resilience it lacked in overt charm. Nothing was quite right, and Freya despaired that she would never find a flower to embody her powers.

In desperation, she took to the skies. Donning her feathered cloak and flying with the power of a bird of prey, she dipped and swirled over the mountain tops, skimming the snowy peaks, and diving between the crevices. At least in the air she felt free and could rid her mind of the worry that she might never find her flower symbol. And it was then, in that moment of release when she had forgotten her plight, that she finally found what she was looking for.

There among the lofty heights, trembling in the chill of the breeze, it stood. Taller than any other, with a strong elegant stem and a flowerhead of the most vibrant violet and blue, a striking color combination to match its chandelier shape. Nodding in respect to the goddess, the stunning bloom was all she could see amid the freezing mists, and so she swooped down to get a closer look. That's when she noticed the shape of the petals, and how they looked like an eagle's mighty claw.

"How unique, how mesmerizing! How can this flower be, in this of all places? It takes my breath away!"

Freya smiled, and in response the bloom seemed to grow in stature and color.

"It is a complicated flower for a complicated woman."

In that moment, she realized she had found her bloom, the flower that would be her symbol and would represent all of the many layers of her psyche. And it would be called *aquilegia*, "eagle" in Latin, a nod to its magnificence and the eagle's claw petals. But in her heart it would always be Freya's fancy, the captivating Columbine, a rare and complex beauty, just like her.

## RITUAL TO BOOST VITALITY AND INSPIRATION

This stunning bloom thrives in a range of different habitats. It can survive at altitude, standing tall, with its star-shaped petals outstretched which often makes it a symbol of aspiration and positivity.

*You will need: Some time and space to relax and perform this stretch.*

- Imagine that you are like the Columbine. Stand with your feet hip-width apart, your shoulders back, and your chin tilted upward.
- Take a long breath in and imagine you're drawing it along the length of your spine.
- As you exhale, picture the breath leaving your body through the top of your head.
- Continue to breathe in this way for a couple of minutes.
- Now stretch up with your hands above your head. Feel the pull along the spine, and up through your neck and shoulders.
- Raise up on to your tiptoes and imagine you're like the Columbine, reaching for the stars.
- Let your fingers be your petals and wriggle them as you stretch.
- Inhale deeply and hold your breath, then as you exhale, let your body relax, and bring your arms back to your sides.

# YELLOW ARCHANGEL
*Lamium galeobdolon*

Yellow Archangel is a large-leafed hairy perennial with yellow tubular flowers which grow in whorls and line the stalk.

**FLOWER MEANING** Associated with protection, healing, and energy.

**FOLKLORE ORIGIN** Europe

## SMELL LIKE A WEASEL

It wasn't that long ago that the world was filled with magic, and that the flora and fauna, and the earth which sustained them, were all living, breathing beings with one common interest—to nurture each other. Nature was more than just a notion, it was a nourishing entity, and those that walked among its bounty were appreciative of its gifts. Every animal, plant, flower, and tree, had a purpose, and a need to flourish and support each other, so the grass was only too happy to feed the cattle, the flowers were delighted to serve their sweet nectar to a variety of winged beauties, and the shrubs produced ripe juicy berries for the birds. It was a continuous cycle that worked with the ebb and flow of the seasons.

The herbs and plants had a use which could be harnessed for the good of others, and each was proud of their special gift. The Lavender, with its velvety violet blooms, lived to soothe those who would inhale its soft scent, the pretty Daisy was a favorite for the animals who lived off the land. It served to add color and playfulness to any landscape. The leathery Mint leaves were fresh and vibrant, and could sweeten the breath and the air, while the Flax, which grew in swathes, was strong and fibrous, and made cloth which the people used daily.

Only one remained clueless to its true talent, a hairy shrub with oval leaves and sunshine yellow flowers which lined each stem. Growing along river banks and hedgerows, and stealing the Bluebell's glory, it coated the forest in a golden glow toward the end of spring. On first glance the plant looked more like a weed, and was often mistaken for the powerful Nettle, but of course this already had a place among the ranks of the worthy. The yellow intruder was known only for its pungent fragrance, which smelt to most like a flea-bitten weasel, and so it remained a stinky outsider and would have stayed that way if it wasn't for the elves.

This pesky faction of the fey liked to cause trouble and defy the laws of the fairy courts, and with the coming of the spring they decided to create some mischief. They had come into possession of some flint, which using fairy magic they had fashioned into arrowheads to hunt with. Then it was a case of finding a target to perfect their aim. The cattle that grazed in the meadows were easy victims. They were slow, and more interested in eating than watching out for fairy pranksters.

The elves were in their element. They'd hide among the bushes and take a shot, then watch as the poor animal fell to its knees, paralyzed by the magical arrows. But while they hadn't intended to kill the beasts, the flint rendered them motionless, and unable to move or feed, which eventually led to their doom. And so what started as a bit of fun became much more sinister, and a problem for the animal kingdom.

The flora, being an essential part of nature, clubbed together, and after much discussion decided they should take action. The elves needed to be stopped, but how could they protect the cattle? While they each had a gift, it wasn't enough to fight fairy magic.

"I can soothe them to sleep, but what use is that?" asked the Lavender.

"And I may be able to lift their spirits," said the Daisy, "but that won't stop them!"

"I could make their breath smell sweeter," said the Mint, "but I don't see how that would help."

"I doubt my fibres would hold them in place," sighed the Flax.

And so it went on, until the clever and powerful Nettle stepped up. "There is one of us who does not have a gift yet, perhaps they can help?"

All eyes turned toward the slender yellow bloom with the tall hairy stem, and in that moment the nameless plant nervously agreed to help. It wasn't sure what it could do, but it was prepared to try.

Spreading its rhizomes in every direction, it clustered around the cattle, providing a protective wall of foliage which swayed in the breeze. The hooded blooms gulped down the fresh air and shivered with fear causing the leaves to unleash their own unique scent. It was a pungent aroma, and extremely unpleasant, particularly for any tender elven noses within the vicinity. And as the flowering shrub rose like angel wings from the moist earth, the elves retreated. They realized there was no way they could get near the cattle, and they certainly couldn't abide the stench. The rooted onlookers applauded.

"You have done it!" cried Nettle. "You are an angel among us, a golden protector of cattle, and for this you will be forever known as the Yellow Archangel."

The flower shimmied from the adoration of its peers. At last it had a use, a gift like all the others, and a place among the Flora. It also had a Latin name, *galeobdolon*, which when translated means "smell like a weasel"—a title awarded for its unique scent which saved the day.

## RITUAL TO RECONNECT WITH NATURE AND PROMOTE HARMONY

This striking flower grows in many different habitats, and as such it sustains a range of pollinators and enriches the environment. Thriving by doing its bit for nature, it can help you do the same and reconnect with the environment.

*You will need: Some time to forage and explore, a notepad, and a pen.*

- You're going on the hunt for some Yellow Archangel. It may be that you know it grows in a particular area, but even if you don't, you can have fun exploring.
- Choose a location like a river bank, wood, or a local park.
- Take your time and wander through the space, taking in all of the sights, sounds, smells, and tastes.
- Make a note of any interesting plants, flowers, trees, and birds that you spot along the way. Once you've found a cluster of Yellow Archangel, find somewhere to sit, and drink in the landscape.
- Breathe deeply and focus your gaze on the bloom.
- Notice any pollinators that visit the flower, and any other insects or birds that come close.
- Take in the environment and what is growing nearby.
- Make a note of what you can see and hear and any additional clues and cues that will help you find this location in the future.

# Chapter 2
# SUMMER

## SUMMER SENSATIONS

As the lazy, luxuriant days of summer linger, and the creatures of the earth bask beneath the sun's glow, so the flowers take center stage. Drinking deep of the fiery rays, they open themselves up and let the heat imbue them root to tip, with energy and vigor. They know that it is time to step into the spotlight, to unleash the glory of each vivid petal and make their stand. From towering Sunflowers with golden halos that they wear like a crown, to beautiful, sweet-scented Roses, that pirouette upon prickly stems. Each bloom within these pages is a head turner: a flower that thrives on the attention. From stories of lost love to tales of wonder and magic, this season's blooms are a playful reminder to embrace the joy of each day and the gifts that summer brings.

# SUNFLOWER
## *Helianthus annus*

Sunflower blooms have broad leaves which alternate along a thick hairy stem. The flowerhead is large and black, consisting of lots of tiny florets. Petals are typically bright yellow.

**FLOWER MEANING** Associated with loyalty, devotion, and happiness

**FOLKLORE ORIGIN** Greece

## CLYTIE AND APOLLO

Clytie was a nymph—a radiant being brimming with youthful energy. She enjoyed playing with the other nymphs in the waters surrounding the city of Athens. Her golden curls would flicker and dance in the breeze and looked like a halo of light around her pretty head. Being almost always in the ocean she was easy to spot, and soon caught the eye of the sun god Apollo. Known for his romantic dalliances, it was considered quite the honor if he decided to shine his rays in your direction, and Clytie was easily impressed. She had never experienced love before and was smitten by his magnificence; it was only a matter of time before they embarked upon a passionate affair.

Apollo adored her innocence and the way she would gaze into his eyes. He felt needed, and that made his head swell with joy. She was a prize, being so pure and sweet of heart, and in return he made her feel special. The other nymphs were falling over themselves for just a look or word to acknowledge their existence, but Clytie had it all. She loved him from the bottom of her heart and would spend hours imagining their life together, how they would fly through the heavens in each other's arms for an eternity.

Those that knew Apollo were wise to his philandering and tried to cool her ardor with their cautions.

"Do not believe everything he says, he has a way with words, and he is much older and more powerful than you."

But Clytie would shrug and flash a dazzling smile. "So? He has never met *the one* before. I am his soul mate. He will not leave me."

Their sage warnings did not deter the nymph. If anything she became more attentive, and would cling to his side each day showering him with praise and adoration.

At first her eagerness was appreciated, but soon it became tiresome for the god. Being the sun, he liked to roam free through the skies, but now wherever he went Clytie would follow. Her devotion made him feel trapped, and he soon began to look elsewhere for affection. This he found in the arms of Leucothoe, also a water nymph. She was older and less needy, which suited Apollo's tastes.

Rejected like the rest of his lovers, Clytie was beside herself. Her dreams had been crushed, and all because of her rival Leucothoe. In her mind there was only one course of action. She needed to get rid of the nymph and reclaim her place at his side. In fit of jealousy she told Leucothoe's father about their trysts, knowing that it would cause a commotion. Enraged by his daughters actions, he snatched her away from the sun god. Some say he buried her alive while others whispered of her banishment. Whatever punishment she suffered at his hands was of little consequence to Clytie. She had removed the main obstacle to her happiness and now Apollo was free to love her again, but the sun god was livid at her interference.

How dare she offend him in this way and take away his love! He needed to do something, to demonstrate his power and show he would not be controlled by a lowly nymph. That said, there was still a part of him that remained fond of her. In his heart he knew that he was at fault, taking one so young and vulnerable and using her as he had. His sense of guilt troubled him, and so instead of ending her life completely, he turned her into a Sunflower. He reasoned that this way her ethereal beauty would remain upon the earth.

The Sunflower, though small and delicate at first, seemed to thrive in her new surroundings. Imbued with determination and a need to bear witness to what the god had done, she began to grow. Her stem thickened and became sturdy in shape. Her head, though slightly bowed at first, began to lift and expand into a broad circle. Shoots appeared at either side, and leaves began to sprout in new directions. Around the upturned dial of her face, golden petals appeared like a halo of light. They stretched outwards and looked to many like the flames of the sun. The Sunflower's brilliance bloomed, and people came from far and wide to take in her glory.

She had blossomed in unexpected ways, but she did not look at the audience that had amassed to see her. She only had eyes for one, the sun god who had stolen her heart and changed her into a flower.

As each day dawned, and Apollo rode his chariot through the sky, Clytie's adoring gaze would follow. Her large resplendent face with its many petaled crown would trail his path through the sky, and she would beam with joy at the sight of her true love.

## RITUAL TO BOOST CREATIVITY AND JOYFUL ENERGY

The Sunflower is a symbol of joy around the world. Its golden hues are a constant reminder of the vitality and vibrancy of the sun. Tap in to this energy with a ritual that encourages you to explore your creative side.

*You will need: A Sunflower, some paper, and a selection of colored crayons or pencils.*

- Place the Sunflower in a vase and take a moment to admire its beauty.
- Think of one word to describe how it makes you feel, for example "happy", "excited", or "energized."
- Write this word at the top of your sheet of paper as a prompt to help you focus.
- Now take your colors and have a go at drawing the flower. This doesn't have to be an exact copy, instead try and capture the spirit of the bloom and draw it in a way that appeals to you.
- Relax and focus solely on the exercise, and letting your imagination roam free.
- Be creative and think of new ways to represent the Sunflower and any emotions associated with it. For example you might want to draw a symbol, or a pattern.

# CARNATION

*Dianthus caryophyllus*

Carnations are a herbaceous flowering plant with blue-green stems. Their fragrant flowers are fringed and ruffled and come in a range of hues.

**FLOWER MEANING** Associated with purity, love, sorrow, and the dead.

**FOLKLORE ORIGIN** Mexico/Korea

## THE FLOWER OF THE DEAD

They called it the Flower of Death around the world, which seemed at odds with the delicate feathered petals, and the vivid hues of the flowerheads. After all, death is a sombre affair, a time for reflection and kindness for the grieving. What comfort could a frivolous form and such vibrant colors bring, except to remind the living of what they have lost? And yet the Carnation longed to be a flower of celebration, of joy and love, like all the other blooms. In some respects it felt short-changed by the powers that be, those who decided the language of flowers and each one's significance. It seemed that lesser-known blooms were appreciated more, and that a plant's beauty was not a factor when it came to its symbolim.

It's true, the Carnation was a symbol of purity, and wearing snow white petals, one could easily see how this association was made. But it wasn't limited to one shade—this was a bloom that could burn

brightly beneath the midday sun, going from hot hedonistic pink, to bold passionate red and everything in between. It cosseted an array of rainbow hues, and many different shapes and sizes, making it one of the most versatile among the floral kingdom. Surely this alone should give it special status, and more positive attributes? But alas, the Carnation's pleas for greater significance appeared to fall on deaf ears.

Why would the flower gods not concede? It seemed unfair to the little bloom, whose head began to nod from the weight of it all. Other flowers tried to console it, whispering of its sweet aroma, and showering its many layered petals in praise, but still the mantle held. This was the flower of the dead, a symbol of loss and heartache, and that's how it remained.

The Carnation could do nothing to change its folklore, and so, deciding to accept its fate, it began to bloom in earnest, emerging in the spring and shining even brighter than before. It puffed out its petals and soaked up the sun's rays. It was a glorious sight, and admired around the world, for who could deny such vivacity. It seemed to all who knew of the flower's plight that it was sending a message to the heavens, saying, "Look at me, am I not a symbol of the living?"

And in the furthest corners of the globe, people were starting to take notice. They had seen beneath the surface, and could feel the flower's unique essence, its bliss at living, at being in the moment and radiating positive energy. The way the colorful bloom captured such a range of emotions, it could almost be human, or at least a symbol of a joyful life. Not only that, it made people smile, lifting their spirits and helping them to recall happier times, moments of pleasure, and deep love. The flower made them feel fortunate for their family and friends, helping them to not only accept their loss, but also to cherish what they once had.

Soon the most colorful Carnations were not only sought, but were lovingly chosen in honor of lost loved ones. Placed in burial sites and woven into beautiful wreaths, they were piled high around the bodies of those deceased, as a symbol of love and a mark of respect. And the dead, though long since departed, seemed to look even more content, as if they appreciated the radiance of the pretty Carnation and everything it stood for. In spirit, the flower imbued everything that was pure and positive about the person who had passed, and the blooms were thoughtfully picked for their variety of hues and what they might represent.

While some countries revered the flower in this way and followed suit, others decided to use it differently to celebrate the living and the dead, for it seemed that the flower had come to symbolize both with its effervescent beauty. Often used in divination, the blooms were placed in the hair to represent the three phases of life—those that wilted first were said to be the most problematic years. The flower was also the perfect gift of love between sweethearts, a message sent from the heart to keep the fires of passion burning. There were the Carnations gifted on Korean Parents' Day as a symbol of love for the dearly departed, and those still present, and the pretty pink Carnations that the Flemish prized and used as part of their wedding rituals.

The little Carnation had over time turned its fate around, and not with animosity or contempt, but by taking pride in itself, and harnessing its talents. The other flowers watched on with admiration for even they had not imagined the power of death, and the delight that one can find in a life well lived.

To this day, the flower continues to work its magic, proving to all the world that it encapsulates so much more than sadness, simply by being the best that it can be—a pleasure to behold, the gardener's favorite, and the precious flower of the dead and those who miss them.

## RITUAL TO HONOR LOST LOVED ONES

Carnations are easy blooms to maintain, and they can brighten up a room with their vibrant hue and sweet scent. They're also the perfect gift, and a way of paying homage to lost loved ones.

*You will need: A bunch of mixed Carnations, a vase of water, a table, a pen, and some paper.*

- Choose a selection of colorful Carnations and arrange them in a vase with some water. Place this in the center of your table.
- Sit at the table, and gaze at the blooms. Imagine that you're surrounded by your ancestors.
- Take a sheet of paper and a pen and write a letter to those who have past. Use the space to say how you feel about them, to pass on your love and thank them for their ongoing presence in your life.
- If you have anything on your mind—any worries or problems— write them down. Explain that you need help and guidance at this time.
- Thank your ancestors for helping to create and shape you.
- Sit quietly and let thoughts come and go. Reflect on what you have learned so far and allow your intuition to flow.

# RED CAMPION
*Silene dioica*

Red Campion is a semi-evergreen perennial. Its leaves are downy and the flowers, which emerge from tall stems, are a deep pink in hue with five notched petals.

**FLOWER MEANING** Associated with care, gentleness, and respect.

**FOLKLORE ORIGIN** Britain

## ROBIN'S GOLD

One of the first flowers to add a glimmer of brightness to the woods each year is the *silene dioica*, otherwise known as Red Campion. A pretty magenta bloom that gets its moniker from the Greek god Silenus, it is a fairy bloom that bears many titles, including Robin's Gold, a name that relates to Robin Goodfellow.

A character from storybooks and a legend whispered upon the lips of children, Robin was a sprite of the highest order. A mercurial trickster and a prominent figure in the fairy world, his name was often mentioned, but he was rarely seen, preferring to slip between the shadows and loiter in the in between. He liked to watch the human folk from a distance and learn about their ways. That's not to say that he didn't enjoy playing pranks upon them. He delighted in exposing their weaknesses. After all, humans were a fickle bunch and easily led. But the secret was to encourage what was already there, to bring out the darker aspects of their psyche and let this be their downfall.

And so, when a merchant journeying across the water to make his fortune found himself at the entrance to the woods on his way to market, Robin was watching. The traveler had been going from town to town, attempting to sell his wares without much success. He was tired and getting more desperate by the minute, for he was a greedy man whose only concern was in building wealth. He had little time for others unless they were of use to him. Being unaccustomed to the area and knowing little of the woods or what might lurking within, he hesitated at the edge, and this pause in momentum was all Robin needed to make himself known. Springing from a dense clump of wildflowers, he bowed low and doffed his cap.

"Kind sir, what a pleasure it is to meet you here! I never expected to encounter such a man of means upon my morning stroll."

The merchant gazed down at the little stranger, and instantly saw a chance to make some money.

"Why it is a delight to meet you too, sir," he smiled, and smoothed the folds of his cloak, in the hope of drawing attention to the fine garment. "I see you are dressed lightly when there is quite the nip to the air."

"Indeed," smiled Robin, "I do not share your wealth, much as I would love to have a cloak as fine as yours upon my back."

The merchant nodded, and stroked his chin thoughtfully. "Well you may be in luck. I am a traveling merchant and as it happens, I have a range of finery that would suit one of your stature. I would be happy to exchange a cloak for safe passage through these woods, and a small amount of gold."

Robin clapped his hands with glee. "What a gracious man you are to do me such a deal, and it's true, I do need a cloak to protect me from the breeze which claws at my shoulders." Offering a hand to shake he said, "It is a deal, sir."

And so the sprite chose a child-sized cloak, richly embroidered, and made of the thickest tweed, and draped it around his shoulders. And then the two unlikely companions began their trek through the woods. Robin, though half the size of the merchant, was nimble upon his feet and as light as a feather, and seemed to drift over the roots, while the older man struggled to keep up.

Keen to secure the money side of the deal, the merchant tapped Robin upon the shoulder and said, "Would it be timely to ask about my gold?"

"Oh yes," Robin grinned, "it is but a heartbeat away. I keep it hidden beneath the Red Campion. It is safe in the shade of the petals. Just a little further . . ." he encouraged the merchant.

Eventually they reached the spot where the Red Campion grew in abundance. The pretty rose red blooms seemed to dance before the merchant's eyes, and he rubbed his hands together.

"Where is it, then?" he asked.

Robin pointed to the flowers. "See for yourself."

The merchant dived in, his enormous hands plunging into the downy spoon-shaped leaves and ripping them apart.

"I can't see anything," he snapped.

"That's because you're not looking properly," Robin smiled. "*My* gold is the sweetest nectar, and the honey that the bees make from it. It is by far the most luxurious of all nature's bounty, and the Red Campion guards it well."

"But what about the *actual* gold you promised me?"

"This is it," Robin said. "If you cannot see its worth, that is not my fault. If you had been a little more respectful toward the bloom, then it might have been more forthcoming. As it is, you have shown little care and deserve nothing."

With that he did a pirouette and disappeared into thin air, leaving the merchant speechless. The man sank to his knees, as he realized the truth of his predicament. He was lost in the woods, with no gold to show for his trouble.

If he made it out the other side, no one knows, for he was never seen again by his acquaintances. But there are those who believe his spirit remains within the coppice of trees, still wandering among the Red Campion in search of Robin's Gold.

........................................................................................................

## RITUAL TO CARE AND PROTECT THE POLLINATORS IN YOUR YARD

This pretty flower is a favorite of bees and other pollinators, and according to folklore, guards their honey stores. Give these creatures a helping hand by creating a bee-friendly yard.

*You will need: A patch of moist soil or a couple of planters, a selection of seeds including Red Campion, water, and a bee box.*

- Rake the soil and remove any weeds.
- If you have planters fill them with compost.
- You can use wildflower seeds, and even vegetable seeds. Bees will help to pollinate your fruit and vegetables and enjoy a wide selection of plants.
- Sprinkle the seeds liberally in the prepared soil or compost and water well.
- Secure your bee box to a wall or fence at waist height. Make sure this is in a sunny spot, near the bee-friendly blooms you have planted.

# LADY'S BEDSTRAW
*Galium verum*

Lady's Bedstraw is a herbaceous perennial with narrow leaves that appear in whorls on the stems. The flowers are frothy yellow clusters.

**FLOWER MEANING** Associated with warmth, comfort, healing, and safe childbirth.

**FOLKLORE ORIGIN** Scandinavia

## FRIGG'S GRASS

When the mighty god Odin sought a consort who would stand at his side as his wife, many lesser deities stepped forward. After all, who wouldn't want to govern with the greatest, the father of the Norse gods and ruler of Asgard? It was the highest honor, and one not easily won. Odin was as wise as he was handsome in his youth, and had his pick of the most beautiful women, but his good sense prevailed, and a pretty face meant little in the grand scheme of things. He was a man of discernment, and while the goddesses fell over themselves to profess their love, it was the one that stood firm and resolute that caught his attention.

Aptly named Frigg, which comes from the Germanic verb Frija meaning "to love," she was destined for that purpose. To those whose only interest was the surface layer, she might appear matronly, for Frigg was not a natural beauty nor did

she have features that could, with a little enhancement, make her more appealing to the eye. She was a pleasant woman with ample curves and a motherly manner, but it was her deeper qualities that interested the god. Odin had always been able to see beneath the veil of things, and when he looked into her sparkling eyes he saw a heart worth having. There was humor there too, and a warmth which comes with age, despite her youthful demeanor.

Odin knew she had everything needed to be the perfect wife and mother, and so the two were wed in a starry ceremony that united all of the realms. Their hands were bound, and their souls too, for marriage meant the world to both of them, and their commitment was strong and true. Frigg soon became heavy with child, and was overjoyed. Her voluptuous curves were made to nurture new life, and as the love blossomed within, so she flourished on the outside. Her skin glowed like the rising sun, her lips and cheeks glistened with morning dew, and her eyes were wide and all-seeing. The other gods looked on with admiration for they had never seen such a womanly beauty, and in that moment they understood why Odin had picked her. Motherhood made her truly magnificent, and because of this she was associated with fertility and childbirth.

The day finally came when Frigg was due to give birth and there was much mirth among the attending maids. The arrival of a new god was something to celebrate, and with such powerful parents the delivery would be blessed with ease. With magic at her fingertips, the birth was sure to be swift and pain free, but Frigg was never one to forgo her responsibilities. She believed in motherhood, and in the rite of passage that every woman must take to reach this goal, and so sweeping her powers to one side, her only request was a comfortable mattress on which to lay.

"But how do we make it both soft and firm?" the maids cried.

"Should we plump it up with goose feathers?"

"Perhaps furs beneath would help?"

"Or maybe satin sheets to cover would do the trick?"

Each suggestion she refused, with a shake of her head or a wave of her hand.

"Do the women that look to me for assistance have such luxuries when they are with child?" she asked. "They do not. And so I will do the same. I am not above them; I am with them."

"So what do we do, mistress?" the maids asked.

"Do as they do, go out into the meadows, and fill your baskets with the honey scented bloom that grows among the thistles. Choose the dried flowers which smell like hay, for they are the softest, and stuff them in my mattress. This will be my only aide."

The maids followed her orders to the letter, piling the flowers known as Lady's Bedstraw, in bundles and carrying them back to the castle.

There they stripped the soft straw-like blooms and placed them in the birthing mattress, ready for their mistress.

The birth was long and arduous, but the plumped-up mattress cushioned the goddess, providing support and comfort throughout, and while Frigg suffered as every woman before her had and every woman after would, the Lady's Bedstraw was a reassuring bedfellow.

Eventually she gave birth to a baby boy called Baldur, who grew to be the fairest of all the gods in the Norse pantheon, and Frigg in turn became known as the Goddess of Motherhood and Marriage, and the deity to call upon to ease labor pains. Standing at the head of the bed, her spirit would encourage women in childbirth, while her flower "Lady's Bedstraw" became known as Frigg's Grass and was stuffed into every mattress to ensure a safe delivery.

## RITUAL FOR A MOMENT OF STILLNESS AND SELF-CARE

Throughout Europe Lady's Bedstraw was a popular choice for stuffing mattresses because of its pleasant aroma. It was thought this sweet scent helped to prevent bed bugs and fleas, and soothe a person to slumber. Tap into this power with a ritual for stillness.

*You will need: Some space to lay, a yoga mat or a rug, and a small pillow or cushion.*

- Place your mat and pillow on the floor and lay down.
- Let your head rest on the pillow and bring your feet toward your bottom and bend your knees.
- Feel your lower back sink into the mat.
- Close your eyes and imagine you are resting on a mattress of sweet-scented flowers.
- Draw a long breath in and tighten your core by pulling in your tummy muscles.
- Hold this position for the count of four, then release the breath. Let your stomach relax and feel your diaphragm widen.
- Repeat this breathing cycle two more times, and on the third repetition increase the count to five.
- Notice how relaxed your body feels as you exhale.
- Let each muscle sink further into the mat.
- After five minutes of deep breathing, give your limbs a gentle shake and slowly raise yourself up.

# IRIS

*Iris*

Iris have thick underground stems and a tall flowering stalk with six petal-like segments. They come in a range of bright hues.

**FLOWER MEANING** Associated with faith, hope, wisdom, and strength.

**FOLKLORE ORIGIN** Greece

## THE MAGIC OF THE RAINBOW

There's a special kind of magic where sea meets sky. It is more than a spectral encounter; it is a moment of divine intervention. As blue merges into blue, and the two become one, the Greek goddess Iris whispers her intentions, for she is a fleet of foot messenger who lives in this space. Sent by the god Zeus as an intermediary between humans and deities, she floats through the ether unseen. It is only when the sun reaches the highest point in the sky and shines brightly through the rainfall that she steps forward in all her glory. Then she is quite something to behold. Her vivid hues blend to form a rainbow arc which transcends the heavens.

It is often said that Iris was one of the lesser gods, a slip of a girl in a pantheon of powerful women. How could she compete with the likes of Hera and Aphrodite? But Iris never tried to be anything other than herself. Preferring to distance herself from petty squabbles, she was happy to serve, carrying jugs of nectar back and forth and offering not a word of judgment, or gossip. She became a channel between the gods, and they would ask her to pass on messages, which she did discreetly. Soon her dedication was noticed by Zeus, who took an instant liking to her innocent charm. Instead of trying to woo her he did something out of character—he gave her a significant role within his court.

"You will be my confidante. You will slip between the clouds, and travel to earth. You will listen to the people, to their hopes and fears, dreams, and desires, and you will tell me of them." He paused. "And if I have a message for them, you will be the one that delivers it."

"But how, lord? How might I communicate with the humans? They are so very different to us, and I do not wish to scare them."

Zeus smiled warmly. "And this is why I chose you, because unlike the others you have a gentle touch, and a kind heart. You will not use this opportunity to gain power."

Iris nodded. "I will find a way to speak to them."

And she kept her promise, for when Iris had news or wanted to give the people a sign that something was coming, she would stretch her glistening wings against the light of the sun and show all of her colors. Her radiance would stretch across the sky in a vibrant parade and those who saw her would bow in awe. As you might expect, the other goddesses were less enamored that Iris had been given such a coveted role. But instead of pleading for her removal, they began to snipe.

"She is nothing but a common messenger," sniffed Hera.

"It is obvious that Zeus chose her because she is lowly, and able to mix with humans. If she were a true goddess, she would be above all of that," laughed Aphrodite.

"There is no need for us to be jealous," they agreed.

But of course they were.

Iris ignored their comments. She knew her work was important, and that Zeus respected her, but more than that she knew that the people loved her. She saw the way their faces lit up at the sight of her upon the horizon, and that made her love them even more. She could feel their pain and pleasure as if it were her own, and she was able to reach out to them.

"Why do you bother?" the other goddesses asked. "They are only human."

Iris would smile to herself and whisper, "They are so much more than that. It is a shame you cannot see, but perhaps I can show you."

To her the humans had qualities she admired: loyalty, honor, and a deep love and respect for each other, which was even more evident in death. Iris desperately wanted to show her empathy and demonstrate to the other deities what being human meant. Being both a woman and a goddess, she decided that she would send them a sign, a simple but dazzling token of her affection to show that she was always there and would guide their loved ones onward.

Every time a girl or woman died, and their body was laid to rest, Iris would kiss the upturned soil at the side of the grave with her soft lips, and there would spring a bloom: a beautiful, elegant flower with deeply colored petals that seemed to be both erect and upward pointing, while also cascading down to the earth. And the people would stop and stare, and say, "Look, see the Iris growing, its colors are like the rainbow. It is a sign from the goddess."

Over time they followed suit, planting the pretty flowers by fresh graves to ensure that their loved one was guided on to the next life by the rainbow goddess, and the Iris became synonymous with strength and faith. Sometimes the blooms were strewn at the graveside, mementos left by those in mourning, but always they appeared as if to petition the goddess to escort the soul and deliver a message of love.

And so the messenger goddess became more than just a serving girl and a lowly deity. She became a treasured icon, and the namesake of a flower that would grow all over the world and become a symbol of great kindness. Wherever the Iris bloomed, it was a reminder of the magic of the rainbow, and of what it means to be human.

## RITUAL TO INSPIRE HOPE AND MANIFEST FUTURE PLANS

Irises produce numerous showy flowers on a single plant to attract a range of pollinators. They're easy to plant from a bulb and require little attention but one glance is enough to inspire and promote new ideas.

*You will need: A space to plant some Iris bulbs outside, an optional trowel, a pair of gardening gloves, Iris bulbs, and water.*

- Before you begin, think about the seeds of hope you'd like to plant in your own life. Is there a goal that you'd like to work toward or a target that you'd like to reach? This could be something specific like passing an exam, or something more general, like broadening your horizons and making new friends.
- Within the soil, scoop out a series of deep holes for each Iris bulb.
- Position the bulbs and gently pat them down, then cover with the remaining soil.
- Water the area well and visualize the bulbs growing and evolving into beautiful blooms. Every time you water your Irises, run through this visualization, and see yourself achieving your goal.
- To finish, think of your own dreams and see them coming to fruition. Try and imagine how you'll feel when this happens.

# DAISY
## *Bellis perennis*

Daisies are a composite bloom with a ray of white petals which surround a central bright yellow disc. Their leaves are oblong upon a long stalk.

**FLOWER MEANING** Associated with hope, joy, purity, and new beginnings.

**FOLKLORE ORIGIN** Europe

## THE DAISY CHAIN

Once upon a time, there lived a girl called Hope—a playful soul with a head full of magical stories, and a yearning for adventure. She lived in a world of daydreams, an imaginary place where anything could happen. While she was young, this was not a problem. Her parents would smile and shake their heads fondly. After all, it was to be expected at such a tender age. But as she grew, so too did their fears, for Hope seemed to meander through life with her head in the clouds. With a glazed expression and a lazy smile, she would skip through her days, leaving those around her exasperated.

"Hope, did you forget to milk the cows this morning?"

"Hope, you left gate open again."

"Hope, where is your head today?"

She would shrug, and with a beaming grin say, "The fairies made me do it," or words to that effect.

"Fairies aren't real," her mother would snap. But Hope would laugh. "That's what they said you'd say!"

Of course there had always been tales about the wee folk, and people were wary even if they said they didn't believe. It was common knowledge that you should never venture out at nightfall on Midsummer's Eve, lest you should meet with the fairy king or queen. Such an encounter would surely end with you being carried off into the fairy otherworld. Worse still, you could be transformed into a Daisy, a fate that was commonplace among naughty children who had wandered off the beaten track.

Most of the townsfolk were blessed with common sense and knew that these were cautionary tales to keep children in check. But Hope thought differently. In her heart she believed in the fairy realm. It seemed perfectly reasonable that children should be turned into flowers if they happened across a mischievous sprite, and if that was the case, there were a lot of foolish ones, for there were hundreds of Daisies in the field outside her house. More importantly children went missing all the time, so who really knew?

There were so many questions Hope pondered, as she wandered the hills and valleys. And yes, she should really have been concentrating on her school work, or the tasks that her parents had set her, but thinking about fairies was far more interesting. And so life went on, and Hope, far from changing her ways, became even more obsessed with magic.

One day she decided to pick all of the Daisies in the field just for fun. If they were the spirits of abducted children, then she wanted to know how many there were. She started late in the afternoon, plucking the tiny blooms from their resting place in the soil as she worked her way up the hill. Time passed quickly, but Hope was so lost in her own thoughts she failed to notice the late hour or the dark clouds gathering. Soon she was at the top of the hill, and her basket was nearly full of white and yellow flowers. It was then that she noticed the sky had become a thick sheet of black about her shoulders.

She could just see the tiny farmhouse in the distance, but she would never make it down the hill before the heavens opened. Her only course of action was to sit tight at the top and wait for the storm to fade. To pass the time Hope decided to make a Daisy chain, stringing the flowers together by their stems. When she was done, she looped it around her neck several times.

The storm was becoming more intense by the second. Lightning bolts split the air in two, and the rumbling thunder made the hill quiver. Hope was scared. She knew that she was exposed to the elements and vulnerable, and yet it seemed that the lightning avoided her on purpose, firing bolts at the surrounding area, but leaving her alone.

She smiled then, as she recalled an old tale about Daisy chains and fairy magic, and how the wearer would be protected by the fey.

Of course it was true! The fairies would not let her down. Clambering to her feet, she began to half slide, half run down the muddy hill. She was getting soaked, but she couldn't wait to tell her folks about the Daisy chain charm. By the time she reached the bottom she was drenched, but still in one piece.

"Ma!" she cried as she burst into the farm cottage. "Fairy magic is real!"

Her mother, though hugely grateful she had survived the storm, was angry that she had been out there in the first place and ignored her protestations.

"I can prove it. Look, I made a Daisy chain charm!"

She grasped around her neck, but the necklace had disappeared. It must have dropped off, and the flowers scattered as she ran.

That would have been the end of it, with no more said on the subject, had it not been for the next day.

They came in their droves—the children who had been missing for years. Some were laughing, some snivelling and rubbing at their eyes. There were those who were arm in arm, looped together as they skipped through the fields. They appeared out of nowhere, coming back from wherever they'd been hiding, all bright-eyed, full of hope, and ready for a new beginning. When asked where they'd been all this time, they simply smiled, pointed to the hill, and said, "We were here all along, in among the Daisies."

## RITUAL TO PROMOTE JOY IN THE PRESENT MOMENT

A tea made from Daisy flowers and roots is often used as a blood purifier, and can help to ease coughs and bronchitis. Wearing a Daisy chain is believed to have a similar healing, uplifting effect.

*You will need: A handful of Daisies.*

- You are going to make a Daisy chain. Lay the Daisies out from flower to stem until you have a rough circle, which will give you an idea of how big your chain will be.
- Use the flexible stems to join the blooms together by twisting them together using loose knots.
- Focus solely on the task in hand, and every time your attention wavers, bring it back to the Daisies.
- Your creation doesn't have to be perfect; some semblance of a chain is enough.
- Wear it around your wrist, in your hair, or hang it somewhere in your home as a reminder to seize the joy from each moment.

# FLAX

## *Linum usitatissimum*

Flax is a herbaceous annual with small, lance-shaped leaves which alternate on the stalk, and five-petaled blue, pink, or white flowers.

**FLOWER MEANING** Associated with growth, intelligence, freedom, and devotion.

**FOLKLORE ORIGIN** Germany

## THE LATE BLOOMER

In a village in Prussia, there lived a saintly girl called Hesta. She was known for her good manners, honest heart, and her ability to pray to the gods. While most of the other villagers believed in the deities and made their weekly petitions, it was Hesta who had the real gift. Through dreams and visions she could speak with the heavenly realm, and that gave her special status among the other girls, but it hadn't always been that way.

Hesta was a late bloomer in all things, sitting silently as a toddler while the other children played and chatted. She watched them crawl and run and seemed quite content to simply be in her spot, unfazed by the world. Eventually she followed suit, much to the relief of her parents, and she even excelled her peers by growing tall and strong. Her height was much remarked upon, along with her thick golden hair, and bright blue eyes. Hesta was a fresh-faced beauty with a kind heart, and she cared deeply for people.

The villagers would come to her door with their problems and ask for help, and she would do her best to advise and pray with them. Sometimes she would lay her hands upon them or perform a ritual to whichever deity was the most appropriate, and they would go away happy and certain that their problems were now being taken care of. Such was their confidence in Hesta's powers.

And so, when the Flax in the fields, which had always grown in abundance, seemed to dwindle, it was Hesta they came to. The crop, which usually flowered in the early summer months, and would then go on to produce a wealth of seeds, had not come into bud. This was a problem because the villagers relied on the seeds, which they crushed for oil, and the stalks for their fibers, which were turned into cloth.

"Have we angered the gods?" they asked. "Is there something we can do to win back their favor?"

Hesta shook her head, in truth she hadn't a clue why the Flax refused to grow. The fields had always been full of the pretty, sky-blue flowers, which seemed to dance upon their slender stems, but now there was nothing. It was as if the plant had forgotten how to grow, or perhaps it was waiting a while before it decided to flourish, which was something Hesta could identify with.

"I will pray on the matter," she said, in the hope that she would appease the people. But try as she might, her polite requests to the nature god went unanswered. She begged for a dream that might shed some light upon the situation, or a vision that could help, but nothing came, and after three nights and many more visits from the worried villagers, she decided to take the matter into her own hands.

Hesta was a clever girl. She knew that the Flax would grow when it was ready and could not be hurried by divine intervention. She also knew that a simple petition to the gods would not satisfy the people, who were growing more disgruntled with her lack of a solution. She needed a grand gesture, something that would placate everyone. After all, if it looked like she had failed to save the Flax, then she would no longer be heralded as the sacred one, and she would lose her special status. It was then that the idea came to her, and she realized the answer had been with her all along. There were two things that singled her out among her peers. The first was her ability to converse with the spirit world, and the second was her lofty height, which seemed to enhance her mystical reputation.

The next day she called a gathering of the heads of the village and told them of her plan. As she described it, the instruction had come from the nature god himself, and therefore they must follow it to the letter to ensure its success. And so a chair was placed in the village square, and upon it stood Hesta, being the tallest girl in the village. In one hand she held a cup of brandy, and in the other a piece of linden bark. Balanced within her skirts were a selection of the finest cakes. She cried out for the assistance of the god and asked that he make the Flax grow as tall as she was, standing upon the chair. Then to seal her prayer she drank some of the brandy, and let the remainder pour to earth as an offering. Then she tossed the cakes upon the ground for the god's sprites, who were known for their mischievous ways, and could help or hinder her mission. Finally, she balanced precariously for a few minutes, as the villagers watched with bated breath. If she put her left foot down, then it was a bad omen, but if she remained steady and true, then the crop would be blessed, and the Flax would bloom.

As ludicrous as it seemed, no one questioned the proceedings, in fact, no one spoke at all. They were entranced by the peculiar ritual and believed in its power. And so a new tradition was born, and the tallest girl in the village would perform the strange offering every year, to ensure that the Flax grew as it should. And of course it always did, for even in those summers when it was a little tardy, it would eventually show its face. Just like Hesta, it was a late bloomer.

## RITUAL TO GIVE NATURE A HELPING HAND AND GENERATE POSITIVE ENERGY

A popular wildflower, Flax is a favorite of bees and other pollinators, which makes it the ideal choice for a wildflower patch. Combine planting with some positive visualization and watch the seeds of opportunity grow.

*You will need: Access to a yard or planter, a pack of wildflower seeds (Flax is usually included in the selection) or Flax seeds, and water.*

- Mark out a patch of land for your planting. If you're limited on space, you can use a large planter or pot.
- Sift through the top layer of soil with a fork.
- Take a handful of seeds and sprinkle them into the soil.
- Imagine that the seeds are your hopes and dreams and feel the potential as you sow them into the fertile ground.
- Water the soil liberally and visualize the seeds growing into an array of beautiful blooms.

# LAVENDER

*Lavandula*

Lavender is a perennial herb with narrow gray-green leaves and long stems. The flowers are lilac to violet in hue and grow along blunt spikes.

**FLOWER MEANING** Associated with royalty, elegance, purity, and serenity.

**FOLKLORE ORIGIN** Egypt

## THE QUEEN'S PERFUME

They called her the Greatest Queen of Egypt, and it's true she was a formidable force, for her actions helped to shape the Roman Empire, and win back her throne. Yet despite her reputation and the admiration of her people, Cleopatra was never fully happy with her appearance. While she was not a natural beauty, her face showed character and a degree of strength. This along with her pale blue eyes helped to win favor with the opposite sex, but it was never enough to satisfy her need for beauty.

When she gazed in to the mirror, it seemed that the prominence of her chin took over everything, and the wideness of her brow only accentuated her aquiline nose. And while some would have been joyous to be blessed with such structure, Cleopatra could only pick fault, believing that as ruler and queen, she should be renowned throughout the Egyptian empire for her magnificence. The angular

lines that exuded tenacity did little to reveal the softness inside. After all, she was a woman, and a passionate one at that. For her to feel truly acknowledged she needed love in all its many forms. And so a lifelong quest to perfect her looks commenced and became just as important as matters of state.

Cleopatra, being a woman of means, had access to all of the latest treatments, and was openminded when it came to trying something new. Her palace was a treasure trove of ingredients, and her quarters could rival any spa by today's standards. She considered herself to be a trendsetter in all things, and luxury was at the top of her list.

From head to toe, her daily routine was delivered with military precision. Her hair, undoubtedly one her most admired features, was kept smooth by extracting the juice of the Aloe plant and applying the balm to her locks. Once rinsed, honey was used to add extra shine to each curl. Her eyes she framed by using powdered turquoise to dust upon her lids, and to add fire to her cheeks and lips, she used a little red ochre. Her skin was super soft, but never smooth enough for her liking, and in her search for the ultimate preparation she tried a number of concoctions, including donkey milk, which she bathed in daily.

It seemed that Cleopatra had thought of everything, for she was exceptionally clever, and a master at manipulation, but while she always looked her best, how she smelt was a different matter. It's not that she was unclean, far from it, but bathing in donkey's milk regularly left a pungent aroma on her skin. Some said it was a little like death, while others simply held their noses for fear of upsetting their queen. The stench, for that is what it was, became deeply embedded in her pores, and would increase in power under the heat of the African sun. By the end of the day it was unbearable to most, but the queen seemed to be immune to the foul scent. Perhaps she had smelt it so often it had become a part of her and would have remained that way if it hadn't been for a young serving boy.

Like most of tender years, he did not know to hide his true feelings, and upon encountering the queen, wrinkled his nose in disgust. Cleopatra was beside herself. In truth, she had known something was amiss when her lover Mark Antony had refused to enter her bed chamber for the umpteenth time, feigning sickness as an excuse. And while she had been trying to work out how to lure him back into her arms, the answer it seemed was in her midst.

Her yards were rife with Lavender, and the pretty purple blooms gave off the most intoxicating scent. She would often walk among the feathery flowers of an evening and inhale the sweetness. If she could smell like this, then it would surely mask the aroma of the donkey's milk, while attracting all manner of compliments. And so, with her mercurial mind set upon the task, she ordered her handmaids to gather an abundance of the blooms and to create a mixture that she could rub upon her body. At first she used the crushed leaves, and then over time she found a way of extracting the oil and applying it directly to her skin. The fragrance was heavenly, and Cleopatra soon found herself attracting many lovers, including the much desired Mark Antony.

So thrilled was she that she ordered the planting of more Lavender shrubs. After all, it would not do to run out of this magical ingredient. But little did Cleopatra know that her sensual savior would also be her downfall, for while the bushes were an attractive addition to the palace courtyard, they were also a draw for all manner of creatures, including the asp that killed her. Loitering among the scented foliage, the snake made its home, waiting for the perfect moment to strike. And as the sun bid farewell, and the moon's dim light cast sultry shadows upon the yard, the asp revealed its slithering form.

And so the Queen of Egypt met her doom, and some might say that it was a fitting end, for one so consumed with power and vanity. But let us not forget she was a woman too; clever, charismatic, and a leader of men. Whether she realized it or not, her magnificence would be remembered, not just throughout the Egyptian empire, but in the entire history of the world.

## RITUAL TO SOOTHE THE BODY AND MIND

Whether you have some Lavender growing in your yard, in a window pot or planter, or in a local park, spending time in the company of this glorious plant when it's in bloom will infuse you with feel-good vibes.

*You will need: Access to a Lavender bush.*

- Find somewhere that you can sit near the Lavender.
- Close your eyes and use your other senses to connect with the plant.
- Inhale deeply and breathe in the aroma. Notice not only how it smells, but how it feels on the tip of your tongue. How does it taste?
- Think of some words to describe it and let the scent imbue you with peaceful energy.
- Pay attention to what you can hear. You might notice the sound of the breeze ruffling the leaves, or the gentle thrumming of bees.
- Follow each noise and notice how together they form a natural orchestra which soothes your mind.
- Open your eyes and take in the beauty of the Lavender. Notice the color and shape. Reach out and touch the leaves. How do they feel?
- To finish, simply enjoy a moment of stillness and let the presence of the Lavender calm you.

# PARSLEY
*Petroselinum crispum*

Parsley is a hardy biennial that has deep green, flat or curly leaves which grow in clusters. The flowers are tiny and delicate, usually light green or yellow in hue.

**FLOWER MEANING** Associated with protection, love, and joy.

**FOLKLORE ORIGIN** Italy

## PETROSINELLA

A long time ago in Italy, when giants and men lived side by side, there lived an ogress. As tall as a house, with dark bulging eyes and a razor-sharp chin, some might say her features were repugnant, but she cared little for their name-calling. She kept herself to herself, preferring the company of plants and flowers. Her yard was her refuge, a place where she could escape into the greenery, and let the lush foliage lift her spirits. She would spend hours tending her herbs, sowing the seeds, pruning, watering, and carefully removing the weeds to give them the best chance at life. In truth, the ogress was not an ogre, simply a woman who loved to nurture.

Living next door to the ogress was a pregnant woman. She was selfish and thought only of herself and her needs, despite being with child. Like many pregnant women she had cravings, and would do anything to satisfy them. The most desperate of all was her need for Parsley. She had never had a taste for the herb before, but now she would do anything to get her hands on the fresh leaves.

One night, when the ogress had taken to her bed, the woman crept out and stole several bundles of the herb from her neighbor's yard. The ogress was devastated. Most of her lovely plants were decimated, and the thief had trampled on the rest of her yard, destroying some of her favorite blooms. Even worse, the fiend responsible had no shame, for she stood in her yard nibbling on the last bits of Parsley leaf. The ogress was livid but decided to give her neighbor another chance.

"Please do not steal my Parsley. I have spent a long time growing it. If it happens again, I will not be as understanding." The woman shrugged. She had little remorse, and the next night she did exactly the same thing! Once again the ogress appealed to her better nature.

"If you take something of mine, then I will have something of yours to replace it!" she snapped. But the woman ignored her. She could not stop stealing the Parsley and took every last bit.

The ogress, enraged, said, "I warned you! When your child is born it will be mine as payment for all that you have taken from me!"

"You can have her! I do not care," she said smirking, for she believed that the ogress would not go through with her threat. But she was wrong.

When the baby was born the ogress appeared. "I will take what is mine now," she said and gently lifted the tiny infant into her arms. The baby gurgled and kicked its legs, as the ogress rocked it in her arms. It was a beautiful little girl with a mass of golden curls, and a Parsley shaped birth mark over her heart.

The ogress traced it with a giant finger and said, "I will call you Petrosinella, after the herb that marks your chest. The flower that sustained you before you were born."

Just like her namesake, the girl grew and blossomed. The ogress knew that such a beauty could be easily stolen from her, and she didn't want to lose the joy she felt in her heart every time she saw her daughter, so she built a tower made from a singular stone column, with a cluster of turrets at the top, and a small window for the girl to peak out. It stood in a clearing within the forest and that's where she imprisoned her.

Every day she visited the girl, bringing food and water and all manner of gifts. She would sit and tell stories and brush her daughter's long flowing locks. In truth she did everything she could to make the girl comfortable, but Petrosinella grew more and more frustrated. She hated being trapped inside and longed to run through the grass and chase the butterflies but each time she suggested these things the ogress would silence her. "I cannot lose you; you are everything to me," she would say gently.

One day a young prince happened to chance upon the tower, and calling up to the window, he attracted Petrosinella's attention. They talked for hours, the prince entranced by her charm, and she enamored by his attentions. Every day he would come, and she would hang out of the window, and he would describe the outside world to her and the adventures they could have together, and they began to hatch a plan for her escape. When her hair was long enough, she would lower it out of the window, and the prince would climb up and set her free.

The ogress was unaware of the prince's visits or her daughter's intentions, so when the day finally came, and Petrosinella let down her long tresses, it was a shock. It seemed that all she held dear was taken from her, and the ogress wept at the cruelty of life.

"I have done my best to protect you, and still you leave me," she whispered through her tears.

As she moaned with grief, a small figure emerged from the trees.

"Mother," Petrosinella said softly, "do not weep. I am still here, but I need to be free." She touched a hand lightly to her heart. "I am like the Parsley that you named me after, I need the air to breathe, the sunlight to warm my skin, and the freedom to grow."

In that moment the ogress understood—just like the plants in her care, her daughter needed to be free. The time had come to let her go. She kissed the tip of her giant finger, and placed it on Petrosinella's chest. "You will always be protected; you have the mark of Parsley upon your heart, and my love sits within."

To this day, Parsley thrives if tended inside during the first frosts, and then allowed to grow freely outside for the rest of the summer.

................................................................

## RITUAL TO PROTECT AND BOOST YOUR VITALITY

Rich in antioxidants, Parsley is packed with vitamin K which protects bone health. Drinking an infusion of this herb can reduce bloating, boost immunity, and help you to feel energized.

*You will need: A bundle of fresh Parsley, hot water, and a cup.*

- Take the bundle of Parsley and spend a few minutes inhaling the pungent aroma of the leaves.
- Close your eyes and breathe it in. Let the warmth settle in your chest and feel the healing power of the herb fill you up.
- Steep the leaves in a pan of hot water for 5–10 minutes.
- Strain into a cup, and gently sip.
- Take your time and let the flavor of the tea dance upon your tongue and enliven your senses. Breathe and relax.

Note: Parsley is best avoided in pregnancy and in acute inflammation of the kidneys. If you are on any medication, use a few sprigs of parsley rather than a bundle.

# ROSEMARY
## *Salvia rosmarinus*

Rosemary is a herbaceous bloom with tubular flowers, usually blue, pink, or purple. They have flaring petals and slender leaves.

**FLOWER MEANING** Associated with powerful women, clarity, psychic ability, and strength.

**FOLKLORE ORIGIN** Europe

## ROSEMARY'S LOVE

Ever since she was a young girl, Rosemary had wondered who she would marry, and how they would meet. Would they stumble upon each other at the village market, perhaps both reaching for the same loaf of bread, or would her suitor be the one serving her? Would she catch his eye, and in that brief moment ignite the spark of love, or would it be a slow burn—a friendship which turned into romance? She had imagined it in her head many times, and it hadn't gone unnoticed by those around her.

"You know there is more to life than marriage, my dear!" her mother would bristle, but Rosemary would simply smile and say:

"I know what I want, and I will get it!"

She knew that she was destined to be a bride. What could be more perfect than finding your true love? She had seen it happen many times. First with her two sisters and then with her friends and the

other young women in the village, and now it was her turn. Except that Rosemary was yet to meet anyone special, although she had certainly tried! A simple stroll through the village was always viewed as an opportunity to meet the love of her life. She would stride out with confidence, her skirts swishing and her heels tapping out a sound that must surely have woken the dead, but it did little to attract the attention of a prospective suitor. If anything, her confidence and the way in which she held herself raised eyebrows, and those who might have given her a second glance had she been more coy turned away.

"I don't understand why they do not look at me! I look them straight in the eye and smile, but they do not return the favor. Am I not pretty?" she would ask her mother.

"Of course you are dear," she sighed, "but perhaps you are a little too much for them."

"Too much? I am simply showing them that I like them."

"Then perhaps they are not the one for you."

"But how do I find them?" she pondered, and that's when she decided to enlist some magical assistance.

She'd heard the old wives' tales, the stories, and superstitions that were passed down through her family. She knew that there were ways to discover the identity of your soul mate—mystical, otherworldly ways. For most of her young life she'd learned the traditions and customs, the healing properties of each plant and flower, and how to use them. And so, on Midsummer's Eve, she decided to take matters into her own hands. She would take a plate of flour as an offering and leave it beneath the Rosemary bush which grew in her yard, and that night she would dream of her future husband. She had always felt an affinity with the bushy herb with its needle like leaves, and potent scent, and not just because she shared the same name. It was riotous, taking up most of the small patch of land, and she admired its strength of spirit. This along with the fact that it was thought to promote prophecy, made it the ideal choice for her ritual. But while the plate of flour was still there in the morning, and the Rosemary plant stood tall and true, the dream she'd longed for did not come.

"I can't have done it right!" she grumbled. "Perhaps I need to do a spell instead." And so the following night she removed a sprig of Rosemary from the bush, dowsed it in sticky honey to attract love, and let it dry on her windowsill. In the morning she attached it to her lapel and went for her usual promenade through the village. The results were the same, if not worse, than her previous efforts. Instead of drawing love, the charm seemed to repel any admirers. Some even scurried in the opposite direction. Poor Rosemary was beside herself. "Am I not good enough for any of the young men in the village? I don't understand what I am doing wrong!" She said holding her head in her hands. Her mother, sat down beside her.

"Have you ever thought that they are not good enough for you?"

Rosemary shook her head. "But it must be me!"

"Why? Because you are a strong, powerful young woman who knows what's she wants, and is not afraid to express herself?"

Her mother took her hand in her own. "They're not good enough for you, because when they look at you they see your strength, and that makes them feel afraid. That is why they turn away. Have you ever wondered why we called you Rosemary when you were born?" Rosemary shrugged. "Well, let me tell you. You are young, beautiful, and vibrant, just like the plant. You are not afraid to be who you are, to break free, and step into your power. When I first held you as a tiny baby, and looked into your eyes I could see that, so I named you after the most powerful, magical herb in the yard in the hope that it would remind you of your strength."

Rosemary grinned; she could feel the truth of her mother's words in her heart. She had thought she needed love to survive, and it was true she did, but not the affections of a man who might dull her light and make her change her ways. The love she needed, was from herself. And perhaps, when she finally loved herself as she deserved, then all other types of love might follow. But if they didn't, it wouldn't matter, because just like her namesake, Rosemary would always stand tall and true.

## RITUAL TO BRING CLARITY AND VISION

This powerful herb has a strong fresh scent which stimulates the senses, helping to clear the mind, and also improvery memory.

*You will need: A small bowl of boiling water, Rosemary essential oil, and a towel.*

- Half fill the bowl with boiling water, then add in five drops of the Rosemary essential oil.
- Place on a level surface like a table and sit in front of the bowl.
- Close your eyes and lower your head toward the steam, then place a towel over the top of your head, to help retain the fumes.
- Inhale the steam through your nose, and exhale gently through your mouth.
- Imagine that with each breath, the steam powers through your mind, clearing away clutter and negative thoughts.
- Continue to repeat this pattern of breathing for five minutes.

Note: Epileptics should avoid Rosemary essential oil. It is toxic to cats, so perform this ritual in a room away from your kitties.

# *Chapter 3*
# FALL

## FALL FLORALS

It may be late in the day as the light fades and the earth begins its steady retreat within, but the fall still has its favourite blooms in those florals that aren't quite ready to give up their turn upon nature's dance floor. They have waited so long for their moment to shine, and even the turn of the season cannot steal their glory. For some, like the hardy Geranium whose pretty petals have seen more than one coming, they have witnessed the birth of each new season. They have anchored their roots and clung to the land, for fear of missing out on any part of nature's spectacle. Then there are those who prefer to take their time and blend in with the riot of colors that the fall will bring. These malingerers are just as important as the first blooms of the year, for they lift the spirits and their stories remind us that change brings renewal and a fresh perspective.

# CHRYSANTHEMUM

*Chrysanthemum*

Chrysanthemums are a flowering plant with aromatic leaves and stems covered in tiny hairs. Their flowerheads are large and showy, often shaped like pom-poms, and come in an array of colors.

**FLOWER MEANING** Associated with love, devotion, and longevity.

**FOLKLORE ORIGIN** The Phillipines

## THE GOLDEN FLOWER

Once upon a time, in the islands known as the Philippines, there lived a young girl and her mother. They lived a simple life, in a crudely thatched hut made from bamboo and nipa, in remote part of the forest. It had been just the two of them since the girl was born. Their only companions were a handful of chickens and the few people who lived in the neighboring village. They found sustenance in the plants and trees and delighted in each other's company. And while there was little excitement in their world, they took pride in their small home, and joy from the quieter moments.

One day the mother became terribly ill. Taking to her bed in an awful state, she was unable to move or speak. All that could be heard was the rattle of her chest and the rasping as she grappled for each breath. Her brow was fevered, and her mouth dry, and it seemed she didn't recognize her only child, such was the sickness that had taken hold.

The girl did not know what to do. She had never seen her mother this way. She tried to soothe her, but nothing helped. It appeared that her mother was lost to her, that the illness was not going to go away by itself. She ran to the nearest village and called for help, but the people were deaf to her cries. They knew little about healing and did not know what to do. Instead they suggested that she scour the woods, in search of the wise old medicine man who lived there.

"He is a doctor of sorts, he will help," they promised.

The girl did not have to walk far, it seemed that the old man had been expecting her. With his long white beard which trailed almost to his feet, he looked at her with sympathy in his eyes.

"Your mother is very sick; I do not know if I can cure her, but I will try."

"What can I do to help?" the girl asked.

The man turned and pointed, "Go deep into the woods and find the tallest Banyan tree. There you will find a golden flower that looks like a Daisy. Pick it and bring it to me."

The girl looked puzzled; how could a flower possibly help? The man simply nodded, "If you do this, you will know how many days your mother has to live by counting the petals upon this bloom."

The girl frowned. She wasn't sure she wanted the answer, but even so she followed his instructions in the hope that while she was absent he would be able to heal her mother.

The journey into the heart of the woods was not without peril. In haste the girl had left unprepared, wearing only thin clothes and no sandals upon her feet. As the night drew in, so the cold wrapped around her skin, seeping into her bones. Her feet were sore and bleeding, torn from the twigs and roots on the forest floor. She stumbled onward, unable to see fully in the darkness. Shadows gathered at her shoulders, offering a glimpse of movement, and sending her imagination into overdrive, but onward she trudged. She had to do this one thing for her mother. Eventually the morning came, and sunlight filtered through the trees to reveal the spot where the golden flower grew. Carefully she knelt down to inspect its petals. Taking it into her hands, she counted, "One, two, three, four . . . five!"

Five days was all that her mother had left. The girl sobbed, cradling the flower to her chest, and then, in a moment of complete desperation she began to tear the petals, at first in two, and then into three and four. She folded them over and over with her nimble fingers. Working swiftly, and pouring all of her love into her work, she watched as the flower responded to her touch. For every petal that she separated, the bloom reproduced even more, and so the bigger ones became thinner and smaller, and layer by layer more glossy petals appeared. Soon what had begun as five became fifty, until there were thousands of delicate petals filling the flowerhead. The girl gasped at the miracle in her hands.

Rushing back through the woods, she ran faster then she had ever done before. The entire journey seemed to take her half the time, and soon she was back at the hut. But instead of finding her mother on her deathbed as she'd expected, she was standing at the door, a broad smile upon her lips. The old man was by her side. Throwing her arms wide she hugged her mother and together they laughed.

"You have indeed done well," the old man said, as she presented him with the flower.

"I can see that it has many petals, and as you will see, your mother is cured! That is down to you and your kind heart."

The girl blushed, and looked at the flower, "It must be magic."

And it was, for the flower was not a Daisy anymore, now it was a Chrysanthemum—an ornate, many layered bloom of intricate beauty, and it would remain a symbol of devotion, loyalty, and longevity throughout the world for years to come.

## RITUAL TO PROMOTE INNER PEACE

The Chrysanthemum is composed of two types of florets, which help to create its puffed shape, along with many layers of overlapped petals. The intricacy of the bloom means there is plenty to study and focus the mind.

*You will need: Space and time to meditate.*

- Create a comfortable haven where you can sit and reflect. You might want to arrange some soft cushions, or light a candle.
- Nestle among the comfort and close your eyes.
- Take your time and focus on your inward and outward breath. Follow the trail of its journey as you inhale, and hold it in your chest, then slowly exhale, letting the air slip from your lips.
- Imagine you have a beautiful Chrysanthemum in your hands (it helps if you have a picture to look at). It can be whatever color you choose, let your intuition pick a hue.
- Picture the image in your mind.
- Look at the thousands of tiny petals that create the flower shape and imagine that each one is a breath.
- Take your time and count each one as you breathe.
- Imagine drawing in the colorful energy of the petal as you inhale, and releasing this into the ether as you exhale.
- Don't worry if your attention wavers, simply bring it back to the flower, and counting the petals.
- Relax and enjoy the meditation.

# GERANIUM

*Pelargonium*

Geraniums are a perennial shrub that is woody and herbaceous, with thick roundly-lobed leaves. Their flowers come in a range of hues, and can be double, ragged, or frilled.

**FLOWER MEANING** Associated with happiness, kindness, harmony, peace, and grace.

**FOLKLORE ORIGIN** Scandinavia

## ODIN'S GRACE

In among the Norse pantheon of the gods, there was one mightier than most in frame and stature, a magician and a poet, and the father of all, known as Odin. Born to Bestia and Borr, he was the king of the gods, and his greatness was celebrated throughout the Viking world. While he had many talents and powers, it was the wisdom which flowed freely through his veins that gave him insight and compassion.

Like anything worth having, this sacred knowledge was hard won, but Odin was prepared to make the ultimate sacrifice. For nine days and nights he hung upside down from Yggdrasil, the Tree of Knowledge, to learn the secrets of the runes. He also plucked his own eye from its socket, in exchange for a sip of water from Mimir's well at the base of the tree. This heady liquid not only quenched his thirst, but offered enlightenment, giving him sight beyond the physical realm, and clear vision.

107

Unlike the other deities, Odin understood the true nature of things and that beauty was in the eye of the beholder and not a superficial construct. As such he paid little attention to his own appearance, and those who saw him often didn't recognize who he was. Appearing like Old Father Time, with long white hair and a trailing beard, he wore a wide brimmed hat which concealed his weathered features and cast a shadow where his eye would have been. From the depths of his cloak he carried a crudely fashioned spear, but even this remained hidden. Odin was a god of secrets, and he guarded them well.

Some might say he was a loner, disappearing for days, scavenging among the rocks and cliffs, and drawing strength from the landscape that had shaped him. In nature he felt at peace, and it was where he went to find solace and escape from the squabbling of the gods, and the demands of his people.

One day, while wandering the hills and meadows, he found himself among a gathering of wildflowers. He had not expected to come this far and being engaged with the present moment and the ebb and flow of his own thoughts, he had lost track of time. His back ached and his joints creaked from the effort of walking for days, and he paused to catch his breath, and rest some weight upon his spear. It was then that he heard the tiny voices beneath his feet, and he glanced down at the pretty carpet of flowers.

"Sweet blooms, forgive me for treading upon your delicate faces," he whispered.

The flowers did not recognize him at first. He looked like a weary old man in need of respite, and so puffing up their petals, they gently cradled each foot to provide some relief. The cooling leaves caressed his ankles, as the heads brushed delicately against his skin. When the flowers finally caught a glimpse of his greatness beneath the veil of his dark hat, they gasped and bathed in the radiant light of his gaze. The deep green foliage softened and splayed beneath his feet, and the little upturned faces of each petaled bloom beamed.

"We serve you, Odin," they said. "We are honored to cushion your steps."

The god smiled. "It is I that am honored by your beauty and kindness."

The flowers, which were Geraniums, bowed and swayed a little for they had never been called beautiful before. While they were certainly a pretty blooms, they were not as showy as some of the others and never normally noticed. If anything they seemed to blend into the environment, contributing delicate flecks of color and a sweet uplifting fragrance.

"We do what we can, but there are others more exquisite than us."

Odin shook his head and bent closer to the flowers.

"There is so much more to beauty than what you see on the surface.

There is kindness, a gentleness of spirit, a willingness to serve others above all else. These are the things that make you truly beautiful, these are the things that give you grace."

He paused to drink in the bloom's aroma, then stared directly at the flowers with his one good eye, and in that moment time stood still. The flowers opened up to the loving look, and for the first time ever they felt seen and understood. Odin's eye twinkled brightly, and for a few seconds it seemed to return to the sapphire glow of his youth. Slowly, under the light of the fading sun and the god's joyful stare, the petals began to change color, turning the most vivid sky blue, to reflect Odin's gaze.

"Now your outer beauty reflects your inner beauty," he said, "and your grace shines for all the world to see."

The Geraniums glowed with pride. They unleashed their natural charm and spread through the meadows and valleys in abundance, and Odin stood tall once more. He was ready to resume his journey and return to Asgard, to sit upon his throne in the realm of the gods, but before he did, he took one final look at the floral carpet before him.

"Such grace deserves its reward," he said softly, his one good eye gleaming with love.

## RITUAL TO BALANCE THE EMOTIONS AND BOOST POSITIVE ENERGY

Renowned for its uplifting fragrance, this flower was revered by the Egyptians who extracted the oil and applied it to the skin. The scent is used today to balance the emotions and alleviate fatigue.

*You will need: Geranium essential oil, and a bowl of hot water.*

- Half fill a small bowl with boiling water and add in five drops of Geranium essential oil.
- Take a moment to enjoy the scent. Stand and inhale the sweet vapors of the steam and waft them around your body.
- Close your eyes and focus on the aroma and how it makes you feel.
- Imagine that with every breath, your body is infused with positive energy.
- Place the bowl in a central spot, a hallway is a good choice as it allows the lovely fragrance to fill every corner and flow easily around your home, but by a window also works.

# DAHLIA

*Dahlia*

Dahlias are tuberous perennials with segmented, toothed or cut leaves and beautiful showy flowerheads which have both disk and ray flowers that come in a range of hues.

**FLOWER MEANING** Associated with inner strength, creativity, commitment, and war.

**FOLKLORE ORIGIN** Mexico

## FLOWER OF WAR

In the desolate, mountainous regions of Mexico, a flower spreads its wings, growing fierce and free as if it were a weed. It bathes the landscape in a riot of color, transforming the earth into a blood red sea, with waves of magenta that pool like the spilled blood of those slain in battle or sacrificed to ancient gods. The spiky petals reach for the heavens, while the tall stems are anchored to the ground by tuberous roots. It is a piece of art which showcases nature's ability to create beauty anywhere.

The flower, known as the Dahlia, is native to this country and born from the dusty plasma of the land. Hailed as the national bloom and a floral treasure, it has a fragrant feisty spirit, but more than that, it carries the secrets of creation at its core. It is said that when the first gods, the sacred beings who guarded this plot of land, came to the earth they used its power to create all that is, and all that would come to be.

In those days the deities had free reign, and chaos ruled. Among those first radiant beings, there existed the earth goddess serpent woman, a snake-like creature with a forked tongue and a feral heart. A woman in shape and figure who could shift into monstrous form when the situation required. One look from her would stop the mightiest warriors in their tracks. She was, after all, an earth goddess and had the power of creation at her scaly fingertips.

The sky gods had pondered her existence for some time, believing she had a greater purpose in the grand scheme of things. The time was coming for her to prove her worth, and so calling for her presence among the clouds, they urged her to do their bidding.

"Take this Dahlia and impale it with the sharpest point of the Maguey leaf, then hold it to your breast all night. Never let it fall from your grip, keep it pressed to your heart so that it may be imbued with the power of creation."

The serpent woman agreed. There was nothing she liked more than a challenge and a way to illustrate her impressive will.

Taking the blood red bloom, she pierced it with the leaf, and then cupped the two together in her enormous claws. She cradled them to her chest. Closing her eyes, she pressed her voluptuous curves into the sooty earth, letting her body merge with the landscape.

Silently, she lay beneath the starry sky. The moon cast a comforting glow which soothed her spirit, but while it would have been easy to drift into slumber, the goddess knew that she must remain alert, holding the flower and the leaf in position until the veil of night shifted, and the sun emerged once more.

It was a long night, and one that seemed to last a thousand years, but the goddess was undeterred. Her skin glistened with the sweat of resilience. She would not let the sky gods down—this was her mission, and she would see it through to the end. Gradually the shadows lifted, and the fiery sun peeped its head over the horizon, and just at that point, the goddess, with all the might of creation surging through her veins, gave birth to Uizilopochti, the god of everything.

The pain was tremendous and all consuming, but the goddess braced herself against the rough terrain, digging deep with her heels and letting the lithe curves of her serpentine form ease the delivery. And there in the burning heat of the morning sun, he emerged from her belly fully formed, a man with a thirst for blood and destruction. For while he was the all-powerful one, he was also the god of war, and this was what propelled him onward. The "eight blood rays" from the petals of the Dahlia had inspired this savage need and imbued the god with a hunger for action.

In honor of this auspicious moment, the flower became a symbol of battle. Etched upon the helmets of Aztec warriors, and carried as a lucky charm, its petals were scattered among the bodies of the dead and used in human sacrifices to the gods. And it grew in abundance, in a variety of forms, becoming a staple in the diet of the ancients. Its tuberous roots were cooked over fires and consumed to instil bravery in the young. Its petals and leaves used in medicines to heal the sick, and it was cultivated for its hollow roots, which were used to transport water over long distances.

The Dahlia had found its place in the world, a habitat where it could flourish and overcome adversity, and this became its medicine. A lesson that it would teach by simply existing. Where other blooms would struggle under the blazing heat, this "Flower of War" excelled in strength and beauty, puffing out its bristly petals and taking center stage in the Aztec story of creation.

## RITUAL TO BOOST ENERGY AND GRATITUDE

Dahlia flowers were once considered a vegetable because of their tubers which are similar to potatoes. They can be boiled and eaten in the same way, and have a spicy, earthy taste. The petals are also edible and have been consumed for thousands of years in brews, soups, and salads.

*You will need: Your favorite yard salad ingredients—such as lettuce leaves, spinach, sliced radishes, a handful of pine nuts, and some olive oil—and a selection of Dahlia petals.*

- You're going to create a yard salad. Wash the lettuce leaves and other ingredients and throw into a large bowl.
- Sprinkle the pine nuts onto the leaves, cover with a drizzle of olive oil, and scatter the Dahlia petals over the top.
- Toss as you would normally, then serve upon the plate.
- Eat the salad mindfully, being aware of each mouthful and how it feels to chew.
- Take your time and notice the different tastes and textures. In particular notice the taste and feel of the Dahlia petals.
- Think about the essential nutrients that you are getting from each mouthful and give thanks to the earth for providing each tasty element.
- When you have finished the meal, notice how eating mindfully has made a difference to the way you feel and how much energy you have.

# MARJORAM
## *Origanum vulgare*

Marjoram is an aromatic perennial with small, spade-shaped leaves covered in fine hairs. Flowers appear in clusters at the end of the stem and are pale pink to purple in hue.

**FLOWER MEANING** Associated with love, warmth, cheerfulness, and a happy life.

**FOLKLORE ORIGIN** Europe

## EFFY'S WAYS

Suspicion and superstition go hand in hand, and never more so than during the medieval age, when people were susceptible to suggestion. It wasn't that they were easily swayed—if anything they were more open to the subtle nuances that life could bring. Changes that were a matter of fate and nothing more, were given greater significance. In truth, life was magical, and each day was filled with wonder if you cared to look, but it was also precarious.

"Things don't happen by chance," was a common belief. If illness or disaster should strike, then it was likely that you had caught the attention of the devil, who was always lurking in the shadows. Daily life wasn't easy to navigate, and some looked for other ways to secure a positive fate.

Effy was one such individual. Everything she did had a purpose, from knocking on wood to keep evil spirits at bay, to never washing on the first day of the year, for fear that she would wash away a loved one.

"I do what I do to keep the devil from my door," she said. She was aware that her strange behavior caused alarm, but as she often quipped when people dismissed her, "I'm still standing and in one piece, so I must be doing something right!"

Some of her practices were questionable, like soaking Marjoram, her favorite flower, in the milk during a storm to stop it from turning, but Effy's eclectic ways were what made her stand out from the crowd, and this she did with gusto.

"She'll never find a husband, behaving like that!" her neighbors gossiped.

"No man in his right mind will stand for such lunacy."

Effy thought differently. She knew there was someone out there who would understand her, it was just a matter a time, and some carefully planned rituals till it happened.

With this in mind, she took to carrying a bundle of her beloved Marjoram wherever she went. She'd heard that Mediterranean women used it in love spells, and she could understand why. It was such a pretty bloom with a beautiful scent, how could it not be used for good?

She stuffed it in her pockets, up her skirt, and in her hair, believing it would attract attention, and this it did in droves.

"It's a charm to bring me love," she said triumphantly.

"You look like a tree!" the townsfolk laughed, but she ignored them and doubled her efforts, adding Marjoram to her belt and up her sleeves. She even placed it beneath her pillow at night, in the hope of dreaming of her true love. And although her efforts went unrewarded at first, soon others believed that Effy might be on to something.

"You've started quite a thing!" the mayor said. He was a portly good-natured chap, and didn't care much for gossip. "Care to tell me more about this pretty flower?"

And so she did, and their conversations were long and full of laughter. Soon the chats evolved into daily strolls and over the weeks and months, love between the pair blossomed. It seemed that Effy's belief in magic was proven right, and within a year they were wed.

Effy wore a long white gown, strewn with pale pink Marjoram flowers and a crown made of the delicate blooms upon her head. The townsfolk applauded and smiled through gritted teeth, many believing she had the luck of the devil on her side. Others were jealous she'd found the one so easily. Then there were those who copied her every move, in the hope that they too might be blessed with good fortune.

Her reputation grew, as did her family, and she was blessed with a home full of plump-faced children. Effy still carried bundles of Marjoram wherever she went, only this time she'd gift them to strangers and those in need, believing that the lovely herb could transform their fate. And while some still poked fun at her curious customs, most kept their thoughts to themselves for fear of incurring her wrath. After all, if she could attract good luck, then it was likely she could incite bad luck too!

The years passed and Effy and her mayor lived a long and happy life, but it was inevitable that the day would come when she would leave the world she loved, and in typical Effy style, she had planned the funeral in advance.

"There will be a row of candles and strewn upon the floor sprigs of Marjoram to keep the devil away and mark my path into the next life."

The funeral was filled with floral abundance, and her favorite flower was at the heart of it all. It lined the stone floor and bathed the coffin in a carpet of pink.

The townsfolk, those that were left and knew her well, gathered, and some scoffed, "Her tricks and rituals couldn't save her from death!" But most were respectful, having been convinced that Effy's ways held merit.

She was laid to rest in the small churchyard, beneath a tall Yew tree, and she was visited every day, for people missed her cheerful charm. If was often remarked how pretty the grave looked. Always clean and tidy, it was surrounded by clusters of sweet-scented blooms. Effy's beloved Marjoram had grown in abundance where she lay. With her for eternity, it became a symbol of a life well lived, and a soul well loved.

## RITUAL TO CLEANSE YOUR AURA AND FEEL REFRESHED

In ancient times, teas and tinctures of Marjoram were taken to ease digestion, and fight infection. It is thought that this aromatic herb can cleanse the body and spirit and boost vitality.

*You will need: A bath filled with warm water, and a sprig of Marjoram.*

- Run a warm bath, with your usual oils and lotions, and place a fresh sprig of Marjoram (including the flower) into the water.
- Let it swirl and infuse your bath as the water runs.
- When your bath is ready, remove the Marjoram, and immerse yourself fully.
- Relax, breathe deeply, and imagine the uplifting energy of this flowering herb seeping into your skin.
- Close your eyes, and imagine you are drifting upon a river, bordered by this pretty plant.
- Let the river carry you onward and let thoughts drift in and out of your mind as you daydream.

# RUE
## *Ruta graveolens*

Rue is an evergreen perennial plant that has oblong pinnate leaves and clusters of small yellow flowers.

**FLOWER MEANING** Associated with grace, clear and psychic vision, and witches.

**FOLKLORE ORIGIN** The Mediterranean

## THE WITCH'S BREW

They called her a witch behind her back. They thought she couldn't hear, or maybe they didn't care if she did. It was true, she looked the part. She was old and wizened, with a hump upon her back and a pointy chin. Her dark eyes were ringed in lines and shadows, and her lips were thin and cracked. Her hair, once thick and black, was now the color of snow, but still long and unruly, so she gathered it in a bun at the back of her head. The Mediterranean sun had taken its toll over the years, aging her prematurely, so it seemed she had been this way forever when in truth she'd simply had a hard life. Now she really was in the final chapter, and her bones creaked with every step. She winced from the pain of her swollen joints. The herbal balms and elixirs she prepared could only go so far to soothe her ailments.

She lived in a small mountain village that seemed to hang precariously on a slope, the white stone

buildings were higgledy piggedly against the vibrant blue of the sky. She loved her home and had created a good life here. It was humble, but it allowed her peace, and time to learn about the herbs and plants that grew on her doorstep and create her cures. Most people gave her a wide berth, and that was fine. They treated her like an animal, crossing the path if they saw her, or turning on their heel. Yet in times of crisis they would knock at her door. Usually by the cover of night, under a blanket of stars, they would come, surreptitiously so none of their neighbors could see, and then once inside her tiny house they would ask for help.

"My husband is seeing another woman. Can you do a spell to help?"

"I am lonely, I need a charm for love."

"My neighbor has put a curse on me; can you remove it?"

On and on it went, each person afraid and in need of her assistance. She was wise enough to realize that what they really needed was an ear to listen, and a heart to offer reassurance. And so she would offer them the same thing, a heady herbal brew made mostly from Rue which she had gathered upon the dry slopes, where it flourished under the baking heat. The yellow flowers were like clusters of gold, with their feathery blue green foliage. There was something magical about the way it spread and added color to the barren landscape, and she would wear it, strung around her neck in a flowery wreath. She knew that it had medicinal properties, but it was unlikely to bring back a cheating lover or attract a new one. Still, it didn't matter what she thought—as long as those who sought her help were happy and believed in its power, then all was well. She had learned over the years that spells were really just a way of training the mind and helping those in need think positively. And while her late night visitors offered their thanks, it never lasted long. The next day they would avoid her at the market and whisper behind her back with their friends, despite the fact that she had been there for them.

But now things were changing. There was a sickness taking over the village. It had started with a young boy who had developed a fever overnight. The following day he was dead. His parents, beside themselves with grief, had looked to place the blame somewhere, and it fell at her door. Soon, as more people were stricken down with the illness, the accusations escalated and the finger pointing became a part of her daily life. She was shunned by most of her neighbors, some even spat at her in the street. One morning she rose to find a carcass left upon her doorstep, the blood from the dead pig was smeared across her door in a cross to suggest she was evil. A lesser woman would have crumbled, but she was strong and wise, and knew the truth. The sickness continued to take more and more lives, but the old woman remained fit and well, which only served to fuel the rumors.

"Why does it not strike her down? She is elderly and weak!"

"It is because she caused it, she cursed us all!"

"She is a witch!"

The only exceptions were those who had visited her recently, the one's in search of magical help who had tasted the bitter brew. They remained untouched by the dreadful plague. Stranger still, was the fact that she could walk among the dying and remain unscathed. It was as if she was protected by the gods—or the devil, as most believed. And so despite the abuse she carried herself with grace and did her best to help, mopping the brows of the ailing and offering comfort where she could.

Soon it became obvious that it was her beloved Rue that was keeping her from death's door. The pungent scent seemed to drive away the sickness, and the flies that carried it from person to person, and the brew she drank revived her. Of course, she tried to tell the rest of the villagers. She urged them to wear the Rue as she did and drink her special potion, but they were blinded by her crone-like appearance and solitary ways and ignored her.

Eventually they all fell victim to the disease, and the woman was left completely alone, although for her there was little change to her life. She would still climb the dusty winding path most days and gather baskets of Rue. She would still make her brew and inhale the aromatic scent from her wreath of greenery. And while she never saw a single soul again, sometimes she thought she heard the ghosts of those who'd lost their lives to the plague, whispering on the wind. They were calling to her with a simple chant that always made her smile: "WITCH, WITCH, WITCH. . . ."

## RITUAL TO CREATE HARMONY IN THE HOME

Historically, Rue was used in poultices for arthritis. The leaves were made into a tincture which doubled as an insect repellent or antiseptic. The herb's powerful scent is thought to have cleansing properties.

*You will need: A small handful of Rue, boiling water, and a strainer.*

- Place the Rue flowers and leaves into a pan of boiling water and simmer for five minutes.
- Strain the mixture and pour the liquid into a small bowl.
- Sprinkle a few drops along your doorstep, and around windows and other outer doors.
- As you do this, imagine golden flowers lining the entrance to your home and attracting positive energy inside.
- Say, "My home is filled with positive energy; it grows like Rue and spreads joy in every room."

# YARROW

*Achillea millefolium*

Yarrow is a strongly-scented perennial with dark green feathery leaves and clusters of delicate white flowers.

**FLOWER MEANING** Associated with healing, love, and inspiration.

**FOLKLORE ORIGIN** Greece

## THE HERO AND THE HERB

Heroes can be born at any time, and in any place. It is the heart of the man or woman that contributes to their valor, and some might say their upbringing. But sometimes a great hero is created by other more magical means. While it's true that the child in this story was given a gift, he was always going to be special. Born to the beautiful water nymph Thetis and the handsome Peleus, king of the Myrmidons, this tiny babe called Achilles was blessed with good looks and even better fortune. Before his birth it was predicted that he would be a great warrior, and a rival for the king of the gods Zeus.

Knowing that her child might be under threat from Zeus, Thetis took action. She carried Achilles to the river Styx, the gateway to the underworld, and there she dipped him into the sacred waters. Holding him gently by his heel, she immersed his tiny body under the rippling surface and prayed that the protective waters would shield him from harm.

"If a blade cuts your skin, may the wounds heal within, and if lightning should strike, may it offer respite. Let it graze but not maim, by the power of your name, my Achilles, my boy, may your life be unclaimed."

As she uttered the words, a transformation occurred. The child within her grasp grew strong, his glistening skin became a shell from within that could not be penetrated. The only part that remained vulnerable was the heel with which she held him, but as she reasoned, who would strike at a man's heel?

And so the boy grew into a man, and a great warrior. He was skilled at warfare, but more importantly he was a kind and noble leader. He fought many battles and left a trail of conquered cities in his wake, and his reputation grew.

While he was thankful for the magical gift his mother had given him, it also played upon his mind. He was an honorable man, and he longed to shield his soldiers in the same way, but how? He did not have the power of the gods and his protection could only stretch so far. It seemed unfair that those who followed his lead into battle had little to save them except their strength and the fates upon the day. To this end Achilles was troubled, but the answer would come during another arduous battle with the Trojans.

Seeking to claim the city before him and add it to his list of wins, Achilles and his men surged the battlements of the city, but things did not go their way. The winds of fate were cruel and many of his best men were slain. Achilles felt helpless. He fell to his knees and prayed to the gods to help the injured heal swiftly.

As he knelt upon the blood-soaked ground, and pressed his face into the dirt, he felt a prickle against his cheek. He brushed away the tears and looked at the tiny plant that had poked from the earth to demand his attention. Feathery leaves splayed outward to reveal a dome shaped cluster of white flowers. He cupped the shrub within his fingers and inhaled the fresh herbal scent. It reminded him of home, of some of the healing salves that his mother had made when he was a child.

Perhaps this hardy flowering plant could be the thing to help? Quickly he gathered a bundle and rubbed it between his fingers to create a soothing poultice which could be placed upon wounds. While he wasn't blessed with the magic of the gods, the love for his fellow men was all that was needed, along with the healing balm from the herb which seemed to slow the flow of blood. Together they worked like a charm. Those who were almost knocking on death's door were suddenly revived, and able to stagger to their feet, and those who were badly injured saw the gaping wounds bind together, and the skin heal.

The herb Yarrow, or *achillea millefolium*, was named after the hero who had used it so expertly, and from that moment on, it was carried into battle as a talisman. Achilles had received his wish; he could protect his men just as he was protected. Except that he was still vulnerable, even if it was the smallest part of his body.

One fateful morning, as Achilles scaled the walls of the city of Troy, the young Prince Paris unsheathed an arrow. With the help of the sun god Apollo, who was enraged by the death of his son at the hands of Achilles, Paris took aim and directed a poisoned arrow to the back of his heel, knowing it would be fatal.

The poison eventually reached Achille's heart and ended his life. His faithful army tried to save him, even applying the herb that he had gifted them in the hope it would work its magic, but nothing could bring him back. Achilles was dead, and his men were bereft with grief.

One thing remained steadfast and true, like the love and respect that flowed freely from his heart—the herb bearing the hero's name. It grew and flourished and continues to do so today all over the world, where it is known as Bloodwort, Soldier's Woundwort, and most commonly Yarrow.

## RITUAL TO LIFT THE SPIRITS AND IMPROVE STRENGTH

While it was used to slow the bleeding of wounds in battle, Yarrow has many other healing properties. Thought to reduce inflammation, it is often drunk as a tea for fevers and colds. It's also believed to boost the mood and reduce symptoms of depression and anxiety.

*You will need: Dried Yarrow flowers, and a hot bath.*

- Take a handful of the dried herb, which you can buy from most health food stores, and either scatter over your bath water, or if you prefer, pop in a strainer, and add to running bath water.
- Immerse yourself fully beneath the water, relax, and inhale the steam which is infused with properties of Yarrow.
- Picture your aura, the energy field around your body, glowing with the bright white light of the flowers.
- See your aura getting bigger and brighter with every breath you take.

# ST JOHN'S WORT

*Hypericum perforatum*

St John's Wort is a flowering herb with deep green leaves and transparent spots. Its flowers are bright yellow and five petaled with many stamens in the center.

**FLOWER MEANING** Associated with spiritual protection, safety, and the sun.

**FOLKLORE ORIGIN** Europe

## THE OLD WAYS

Among the Celtic tribes that settled in early Europe, there was one that made their home in the deep luscious valleys of central France. Their tiny village comprized of a cluster of roundhouses, built with wood and thatch, and furnished with hay and animal skins. While they enjoyed the simple life, they still followed the traditions of their forefathers, seeking answers among the stars, and looking to the animals for sustenance and insight. Sacrifice was a huge part of their practice and a way of predicting the future. Animals would be slaughtered over slabs of stone, their entrails displayed in a pattern that could predict what was to come. The flow of their blood could also show the way of things and was used in rituals to secure a positive outcome.

Their leader Cathal was an obstinate man. The old ways meant everything to him, and while some of his people had formed the opinion that sacrifice was barbaric, he was not swayed.

"This is the way of things; it has always been the way of things and it will not change."

"But could we not look to the land, to make things better?" asked his daughter Brianna. "I have heard talk from tribes across the sea that flowers and herbs can do more than healing. They can predict the future too."

"That is hearsay, and we are *not* the other tribes!"

The conversation ended, as it had done many times, but Brianna like her father was not one to give up easily. She knew in her heart that there was a kinder way to work with nature. Whenever her chores were finished for the day, she would slip away to the nearby woods and gather herbs and flowers. She would hold them in her hands, imagining the power that seeped from each swarthy stalk or stem. She would press the leaves to her head and feel their velvety coolness clear her mind. She would take the delicate petals and roll them between her fingers to release the sweet scent, and breathe it in and feel the magic inside.

Brianna was a natural seer: a mystic who had the ability to work with nature's gifts and determine the future. Her skills were not something that anyone could learn, they were a part of her, but her father didn't want to acknowledge this gift, believing instead that Brianna would make a good wife to the next clan leader. And so the girl pretended to be what her father wanted and practiced her art in secret.

One day, there was a commotion in the village, as word of a great storm spread through the settlement.

"It is going to be a beast," the villagers said. "It comes from the East, and it brings death."

"Our huts will not withstand this."

"We must pack our things and find a new place to live, somewhere that the storm cannot reach us," ordered Cathal.

"But where will we go?" they asked.

Cathal grunted and said, "Pack your things, take what you can carry and leave what you can't."

In truth, he didn't have an answer. He had consulted the stars and prayed to the gods. He had looked to the entrails of both crows and goats, but nothing spoke to him. He had begged for a sign, from the direction of the blood, but it only pooled at his feet. Brianna had fled to the woods in search of insight. Sitting within a glade of Oaks, she closed her eyes and asked for a vision, and the gods responded, for when she awoke from her trance, she saw that the ground was bathed in sunshine. On closer inspection she could see that the golden specks of light were tiny star-shaped blooms known as St John's Wort.

"You are like sunlight," she smiled, "and what better antidote to a raging storm than the sun in all its glory". In that moment she realized what the gods were trying to tell her. The St John's Wort would light the path with its pretty golden flowers and lead them to a safe place.

Scooping up a handful, she ran back to the village.

"Father, you must trust me. I know where we need to go."

Taking his hand in hers, she led him and the rest of her people through the woods, following the path of the flower.

On and on they trudged through the valleys, as the winds whipped at their feet. The sky darkened and the last of the day's sunlight was swallowed by the gathering thunderclouds. Eventually they reached a sheltered enclave, where the St John's Wort also stopped. Taking refuge in the caves, they huddled together while Brianna scattered the herb across the threshold. "It will protect us, from the thunder," she said.

That night the storm raged, but the people of Brianna's tribe were untouched. The sanctuary they had found kept them safe from harm, until the bad weather passed.

Cathal was overjoyed; his people were safe, and his daughter had proved that she was a gifted seer. From that moment on he opened his heart to new ways of doing things. The rituals he'd favored became a thing of the past and he learned to work with the plants and flowers and harness their power when looking to the future. The St John's Wort that had saved the day became a treasured bloom to the Celtic tribes: a symbol of the sun and a charm to keep harm at bay.

## RITUAL TO BOOST HAPPINESS AND INNER PEACE

This aromatic flower is often dried and used in teas and tinctures to soothe body and mind. It's particularly good for alleviating anxiety.

*You will need: A tea infuser, a cup, 2–4 teaspoons of the dried St John's Wort, hot water, and honey or sweetener.*

- Fill the tea infuser with the dried herb and pop it in your cup. Cover with boiling water and leave for at least five minutes to infuse.
- Remove the infuser carefully from the hot water.
- Take a spoonful of honey or sweetener and stir into the cup slowly.
- As you stir, visualize yourself sitting in a field of St John's Wort.
- Inhale the sweet aroma of the steam from your cup.
- Enjoy sipping the tea and continue to visualize yourself in that happy place, surrounded by beautiful blooms, and bathed in the warm glow of the sun.

Note: Because St John's Wort supports the liver in detoxifying the body, it can make certain drugs digest more quickly. As a result, St John's Wort should certainly be avoided by anyone taking anti-rejection drugs after an organ transplant.

# NIGHTSHADE
## *Atropa belladonna*

Nightshade is a perennial plant with oval-shaped leaves and bell-shaped blooms that are purple to green in coloration.

**FLOWER MEANING** Associated with danger, deception, beauty, witchcraft, and death.

**FOLKLORE ORIGIN** Italy

## BELLADONNA

Among Venetian ladies of influence during the Renaissance, a degree of luxury was not only expected, but required. Should you be lucky enough to frequent fashionable circles, then you were compelled to uphold specific standards. No gown was too rich in color or fabric, no scent too overladen with musky sweetness. Jewelery was refined to a point, but not without flair and design, and gold was in abundance.

As a woman, the way you held yourself was key, and even if you couldn't afford the most opulent outfits, you could pretend to be someone, just by using your walk and general demeanor. The most important thing was to maintain an air of authority, but this should be coupled with a hint of frivolousness—after all, you were in the city of love, and a multicultural metropolis. As Venice was a hub of migration there was a continuous flow of commodities from around the globe, from exotic and pungent spices to the most salacious pigments and dyes. It was a cultural mix of extravagance and amusement that attracted the rich in droves.

Most common of all, was the belief that beauty was skin deep. If you couldn't pamper or preen it to perfection, then you must resort to more radical, and somewhat esoteric, practices, because above all else, you needed to be beautiful. And so the women of high standing were always trying to outdo each other in the style stakes.

The latest whisper among those in the know was of a magical flower that could change the shape of the eye and make you virtually irresistible to the opposite sex. The plant known as Nightshade was recognized for its purple bell-shaped blooms, but it was not an easy find, nor was it talked about openly because of its dark reputation. There were those who wouldn't even say its name, for fear that they would invoke the devil. Some believed that its Latin moniker meant "beautiful woman," and it was said that drinking the plant's juice could invoke such a being. After all, this was the witch's bloom, and also a common ingredient in flying spells. But for Bella, a newly arrived woman of substance recently introduced the higher echelons of society, this did little to faze her. She wasn't scared by hearsay. All she cared about was climbing the social ladder. It wasn't that she wasn't gifted in the looks department—she was tall and willowy, attractive by most standards—but Bella longed to stand out. To take her place at the head of the table, and show those Venetian ladies that she was a force to be reckoned with and the truest beauty among them.

And so she commandeered a cutting from the plant, with the intention of harvesting its unique magic. Just a little dab of the leafy secretions to the inner eye should do the trick, enhancing the dark of her pupil, and making it grow in size. Taking her time, Bella applied the juice. She was excited to see the results and couldn't wait to find out what her peers made of her new look. She would surely be the Belle of the Ball, and the most admired woman in Venetian society.

It only took a few minutes for the plant's poison to set about its mischief. It started with an icy cold tingle which spread through the iris, causing her eyes to glaze over. It was alarming at first, like looking through a filmy gauze. Bella could only make out shapes and movements. It seemed that all the sharp edges had been glossed over. Then her eyes began to water, and the chill turned to a fiery heat. She tried not to panic, but the pain was excruciating, so in desperation she dipped her painted face into the nearest water bowl, but nothing would soothe the burning. She wanted to scream, but it seemed the words were lost in her throat. She fell to the floor, and rubbed voraciously at her eyes, but that only made it worse.

Gulping down the air, Bella tried once more to calm herself, and it was then that she saw a spectral mist rising from the ground. Trying hard to maintain focus, she watched and waited until the fog before her eyes lifted to reveal a beautiful woman standing above her.

"Who are you?" asked Bella, shaken.

The woman's ruby red lips stretched to reveal a row of pointed teeth.

"I am what you seek, am I not?"

Bella shook her head. "I only wanted to make myself more beautiful."

"Yes. And I am here to grant your wish, for there is nothing more beautiful than a woman in death."

Bella backed away, but she could crawl no further, and instead curled into a tiny ball. The spectral vision threw back her head and laughed.

"You cannot escape me. I am you, and you are me now."

And with that she wrapped her ghostly arms around Bella's shivering form and squeezed her last breath from her.

When they found her, her body was twisted like a coiled spring and far from beautiful. The Nightshade's deadly poison had acted swiftly, and there was nothing that could be done. The rumors spread among the wealthy and those of influence, and it was common knowledge that in seeking perfection Bella had found death. While most agreed this was what she deserved for indulging her vanity, there were those who appreciated her reasons, for it is only in the eternal sleep that we are truly admired and held above all others—and in that, she got her wish.

## RITUAL TO PROMOTE REJUVENATION

Deadly Nightshade was a common poison during the Middle Ages, but it has since been reinvented. Small amounts are used in medicinal remedies for Whooping Cough, and as a muscle relaxer. The plant is a balance of light and dark, and linked to death and rejuvenation.

*You will need: A sheet of paper, a pen, and colored pencils.*

- You're going to create an image to help you focus your intention for rejuvenation. Take the paper and draw a line a quarter of the way up.
- Shade in brown, beneath the line. This area represents the earth, and your roots. In this space write a list of things that keep you balanced and grounded, for example, "family."
- Above the line is the sun and sky. You might want to draw these into your picture. This space allows you to grow, just like the Nightshade emerging from the soil.
- In this space you're going to write things that help you feel rejuvenated, for example, "learning something new."
- Place the image somewhere that you can see it every day and be sure to practice a balance of things from below and above the line.

# ROSE

## *Rosa rubignosa*

Roses are perennials with prickly stems and glossy green leaves. Their beautiful flowers come in a range of sizes and hues, and have overlapping petals.

**FLOWER MEANING** Associated with love, passion, adoration, and devotion.

**FOLKLORE ORIGIN** Persia

## THE NIGHTINGALE AND THE WHITE ROSE

In ancient Persia, the bird that was revered among all others for its gentle beauty and soulful song, was the tiny nightingale. A delicate creature, with the voice of an angel, it came to represent the human spirit, and was an enduring symbol of eternal love. And while people spoke of this delightful bird, and saw it as an omen of good fortune, they also knew of its sorrow, for it was this that colored its song with sentiment, making it all the more memorable.

The nightingale may have been small, but it had a huge heart. While other birds would flit from bloom to bloom, easily charmed by a bright hue, or a patterned petal, it only had a voice for one. The nightingale was madly in love with the white Rose. Never had it seen such beauty in flower form. It was more than the perfect shape of the bud, or the strength of its stem, more than the honeyed aroma that wafted upon the breeze, or the elegance with

which it held itself. There was something otherworldly about the bloom, a purity that gave it poise and grace, and the nightingale was smitten.

Every night it would perch beside the Rose and look on adoringly. It would puff out its tender chest, and drinking deep of the evening air, it would serenade the bloom with the softest, sweetest melody. It would sing its heart out, using the power of each carefully placed chirrup and note. And the Rose would listen in earnest. It would bend and sway, and dance to the nightingale's tune. And while it never expressed any emotions of its own, the Rose was truly appreciative, and that was all the little bird needed, for it was not like its kith and kin and did not require worship or thanks. It simply loved to sing, and to share this joy with the object of its affection. But it hadn't always been that way.

When the bird had first emerged from its nest, flying solo in the world of humans, nothing more than a croak had issued forth from its beak, and no matter how hard it tried, its song just would not come. It had taken inspiration from the plants and the trees, from the changing of the seasons, and even the elements, but nothing could stir a tune from its breast. The nightingale was barren of music, and would forever have remained that way, if it hadn't been for the white Rose. It was love at first sight for the little bird, and while normally he would have strained to unleash some kind of response, when he saw the flower standing in solitude, his heart swelled, and the fluted notes poured from within.

And so the union between the two was born, and they were rarely apart. As the light of sun burned through the sky, the nightingale would bare its soul to the one it loved.

There were those who scoffed at the pairing, and belittled the devotion of the bird, believing it was deluded. After all, the Rose was a flower by any other name. It had petals, not feathers, so how could the feelings be mutual? But none of this mattered to the nightingale. Love could transcend shape and matter to become something more spiritual, as it had done with them. And so it continued with its wooing, believing that inevitably romance could help it win favor with this fair flower, which it did eventually.

One evening during the month of July, the bud that had been so tightly packed and pent up with emotion began to open wide when it heard the nightingale's song. It had been a natural process, but the bloom had finally surrendered her heart, and the little bird was overjoyed. It danced from leaf to leaf, its voice summoning the deities from their sleep. It clasped the beautiful flowerhead to its chest and sang so that all the world could feel its passion, and in that one glorious moment it held the Rose so tightly, that one of its sharpest thorns punctured the bird's fragile heart.

It was a fatal move that caused the blood to flow. The ruby red droplets tainted the snowy petals of the open Rose, turning them a deep crimson in color, and as the little bird gave up its last breath, the white Rose became red, and the nightingale sang no more.

But while that could have been the end of the story, and a mournful one at that, there is more to this tale than meets the eye. For the Rose swiftly became a symbol of true love, synonymous with romance in its many guises. It was the flower of lovers, and the tradition of gifting Roses became a way of honoring the bird that had remained true to its heart. And although nightingales still sing as sweetly to this day, and all over the world, there never was, and never will be, a love like that between the tiny nightingale and his white Rose.

## RITUAL TO OPEN YOUR HEART AND PROMOTE THE FLOW OF LOVE

Roses symbolize love, and can help you feel more loving by activating your heart chakra, the energy center associated with emotions. This ritual harnesses their energy through color, texture, and scent.

*You will need: A handful of your favorite colored Roses, a paper towel, a rubber band, twine, a clothes hanger, a decorative bowl, and Rose essential oil.*

- Lay the Roses on the paper towel, and select some of the newest, freshest buds, and flowerheads from the remaining flowers.
- Take your time, and make this an exercise in mindfulness, so look at the size, shape, texture, and color of each bloom.
- Carefully dab any excess moisture from the petals. Gather the bundle together by the stems and use the rubber band to secure them together.
- Take the twine and tie it around the end of the stems, then attach this to the base of the clothes hanger.
- Position in your wardrobe so that the Roses are hanging upside down. The flowers will make your clothes smell sweet and infuse them with loving energy, and the dark environment will help them dry naturally.
- After 2–3 weeks remove the blooms, then separate the petals, which should be nicely dried.
- Add them to the bowl and add in a couple of drops of Rose essential oil to bring out the lovely aroma.
- Leave the potpourri somewhere central in your home, so that you can inhale the uplifting scent and connect with the loving energy of this bloom.

# LOTUS
## *Nelumbo nucifera*

Lotuses are long-stemmed aquatic perennials with broad floating leaves. Their fragrant flowers are large, usually bright pink or white, but there are some blue, purple, and yellow varieties.

**FLOWER MEANING** Associated with rebirth, spiritual enlightenment, resilience, and purity.

**FOLKLORE ORIGIN** Egypt

## THE BRINGER OF LIFE

In the beginning, there was nothing. The earth as it is today was an idea, a concept that would blossom over time. The primal waters of existence were all that could be seen, and they were vast, covering every piece of the planet. Stormy and troubled, these seas rippled with every dark imagining, for they were the essence of creation and could therefore be both good and bad.

Known as Nun by the ancient Egyptians, this fluid reality was not a place that anyone would want to be, but humans were yet to be created and so the tumultuous waves carved their own path, crashing against the rock beneath, and cutting shapes into the earth. Whether they had an idea in mind it is hard to say, for Nun was considered a being, a godlike deity who carried many forms. As such he had the power to do anything, but he loved the unruliness of disorder, and so let the primal ocean chip away at the land. Should any type of lifeform rear its head, then the waters would eradicate it, clawing at the very roots and squeezing the life from its veins.

Chaos reigned, and would have done for an eternity, had it not been for the humble Lotus flower. How it started to grow no one knows, for there is mystery to be found at the heart of this bloom and a story that inspires resilience, and the power of life and death.

From deep within the murky depths of the primal waters emerged a mound of earth, so small and insignificant that it went unnoticed at first. Perhaps it would have come to nothing had it not been for the angry seas that thrashed relentlessly, slicing away at the land. Over time the small mount grew in size, rising up gradually in a quest to meet the sky and within its oily depths there was a seed, a single, solitary morsel of life, that began to germinate.

Eventually the seed sack sprouted, and roots began to push down into the mud, anchoring themselves deep in preparation for what was to come. Slowly a tiny seedling rose upward, forcing its way through the damp soil, never giving up, despite the waters that battered at it like a thread in the wind. Soon this tendril of new life began to grow and gain thickness, picking up speed as it maintained shape and form. A flower was evolving, and the primal waters could do nothing to stop it, for while the ocean was filthy, and bleeding with negativity, this was a hardy bloom, a plant that could withstand the elements.

Soon leaves appeared, at first in a flurry that settled around the base, and then slowly a second flourish brought more. These were big and broad, and they floated upon the water as the shoot grew upward.

Nun, being the god of nothingness, watched with consideration. He realized there was little he could do to prevent the bloom from reaching fruition, which it did in a stunning display of strength over adversity. The flower with its wide bright starry petals, took center stage. It shone among the darkness and as the large bud finally opened and the petals unfurled it seemed that the Universe rejoiced. Rays of light, glorious and golden, flowed from within its core, and the sun god Atum, who was only a boy at that time, stepped forth from the bloom. While he may have been in his infancy he was still a vibrant ball of heat and light and his energy swept over the Earth, consuming the primal waters.

As his fingers stretched and flexed in the air, the boy unleashed his creative powers and the gods Shu and Tefnut were born, but before he could do or say anything the siblings were gone, carried away by the ocean. The boy god looked on in horror, but it was short-lived, for the deities were also gifted. Shu was the force of preservation and dry air, and Tefnut, the moist, corrosive air of change which sits at the heart of time. Together these two fundamentals of human existence had the power to overcome the void of Nun and navigate the sludgy waters to return to their creator.

As they stood at his side, Atum was so overcome with joy that he began to cry. The tears that fell to the ground became the first humans. At last the world had begun to take shape, and each change brought new life, which in turn brought love. Eventually the sun god grew into a man known as Ra, or Atum-Ra, and he was worshipped for his all-encompassing strength and benevolence.

And through each twist and turn of fate, the humble Lotus bloomed. It followed the path of the creator god and watched his every move. It rose from the waters of the Nile each morning to greet the sun, and raised its face toward the heavens, bathing in the light of its bounty. Then every evening it dipped beneath the watery surface to sleep. The bringer of life and a symbol of renewal, rebirth, and resilience to the Egyptians. The Lotus remains an inspiration to all, and proof that beauty can be born from darkness.

## RITUAL TO HARNESS INNER STRENGTH AND IMPROVE FLEXIBILITY

The Lotus position in Yoga is inspired by this formidable flower. It can take a while to master this advanced position, but similar benefits can be achieved by a simpler pose which aligns your posture and allows the energy to flow.

*You will need: A comfortable space to sit on the floor, and loose clothing.*

- Sit on the floor, in a crossed leg position.
- Ensure that your head and back are straight, your shoulders are back, and your chest is forward.
- Breathe deeply and rest your hands palm upward on each knee.
- Bring your thumb and index finger together to form an "O" shape.
- Take a long deep breath in, and as you release this breath slowly through your mouth, press down lightly with back of your hands, pushing your knees toward the floor.
- Hold this position for a few seconds, then relax and repeat the manoeuvre with each breath.
- This simple exercise improves flexibility, focuses the mind, and helps to build resilience.

# FOXGLOVE
## *Digitalis purpurea*

Foxgloves have tall flowering spikes which grow up to 6½ feet (2 meters). The blooms are tubular shaped, pinkish purple in hue, and have deep crimson spots at the opening of each flower.

**FLOWER MEANING** Associated with intuition, women's magic, and creativity.

**FOLKLORE ORIGIN** England

### THE VIXEN'S SLIPPERS

"Tread carefully amid the Foxgloves my dear," he would say to his scarlet haired girl, and she would gaze wide-eyed at her father and reply:

"For I enter the fairy realm," and together they would laugh as he hoisted her onto his shoulders.

She had heard the tales many times, the rhymes and riddles he would spin about the fey, and how they lived among the fluted blooms.

"It does not do to annoy the little people," he would whisper. "They may be small, but they have great powers."

Of course, that did not deter her. If anything her father's storytelling had piqued her interest. As a child she was curious by nature and longed to see one of these winged wonders for herself. She'd venture into the woods, full of anticipation that she might encounter one. She would play among the wildflowers, go in search of fairy mushrooms, and

climb the trees in the hope that she might spot a fairy flitting in between the branches. She would run through the tall grasses and emerge dusted in grass seeds, her dress smeared in mud, her hair a tangle of twig and leaf. Then she would skip home to her father tattered and torn from her adventures, her red curls threaded with flowers and other tiny creatures of the forest. And although he loved her dearly and wanted her to express herself, he worried, too. He could see that her true nature was feral, and others had noticed.

It wasn't long before the whispers began: the secretive chatter and side-looks from the villagers who disapproved of her demeanor.

"Have you seen the way she behaves? It's not ladylike the way that girl roams the woods like a savage animal!" they would mutter.

"How disgraceful!" they would say.

But the gossip didn't stop her—if anything it fuelled the fire within, for she was never going to conform to their rules. Being immersed in nature made her feel alive. She would breathe in the musky sweet air, and hum along with the melody of the birds. And all the time she longed to see a fairy, to enter their world and experience the magic firsthand. Then one day, she did.

It wasn't quite how she expected, and it was in a moment of need. She had spent the morning making Daisy chains and gathering pretty pebbles, and now her head was steeped in daydreams. She heard them before she saw them—a group of local youths, almost adults like her, but these were young men seeking trouble. She could tell their true intentions from the noise they made as they plundered through the flowers. It soon became obvious it was her they were hunting.

"Where is the dirty beast?" one of them cried.

"Look!" the first lad screamed. "I see her, I see her red hair!"

"Get her!" they yelled.

But in truth, they weren't quick enough. They stumbled in her direction, their feet catching on tree roots and sliding over the damp moss, and this gave her a head start. With the breeze at her heels she sprinted toward the other side of the forest, to the glade where the Foxgloves grew. A cluster of spears with soft purple blooms bowed in her direction, as if to welcome her. It seemed to her that the fairies were her refuge, and that she needed their magic more than anything. She gazed intently at the flower, taking in the beauty of its pattern and form.

"Help me, sweet fairies. Keep me safe from harm."

Within seconds, a beautiful gossamer-winged being appeared, with large almond-shaped eyes and golden hair. The fairy didn't say much, instead it spoke to her heart and mind, and with a slender ethereal finger, pointed to the flowers. Immediately she understood, she must hide among their tall spires, and that she had permission to enter the realm of the fey. She stepped into the center of the cluster and crouched in a small ball. As she did, something strange happened. Her skin began to tingle, her body trembled, and she diminished in size. Her twinkling eyes became dark and bright, and she could see everything. She could smell every strand of scent, and she could hear the snap of trampled stems, as the youths approached. The fairy had promised to hide her, but the Foxgloves offered little protection from the boys' hungry eyes. She held her breath, as her eyes met one of her abusers. And then he spoke.

"Look," he said, shaking the others. "There's a fox. Looks like a vixen."

The youths muttered something, but the leader shook his head. "No, we haven't time to bother with it. She must have ran over the fields." He turned swiftly and loped off in the other direction with his gang in tow.

The girl, who was now a fox, released a breath, and took a couple of tentative steps upon her new paws. She moved out beyond the Foxgloves, and as she walked she noticed that some of the fallen flowerheads had become slippers, gently covering her feet. "How odd!" she thought, and yet it seemed like she was dancing on air, padding so gracefully that not a soul, human or otherwise would be able to hear her coming. She liked this new shape, the strength in each stride, and how she could leap through the air. She was finally able to run with the fairies, to spend her days in their company and her nights beneath the stars.

As for her father, he had always known she would leave one day. He'd always encouraged her to be true to herself, so while he was saddened that she didn't return, he knew in his heart that she was away with the fairies, and that made him happy. And, as it turned out, he wasn't completely alone. Some evenings he was visited by a beautiful red vixen, who would sit by his feet as he told his stories.

## RITUAL TO BOOST POSITIVE ENERGY

Foxgloves are poisonous, and care should be taken when handling them, as they can cause an allergic reaction, so it's better if you can admire from a distance in the wild. Even so they're full of magic, and can help you feel more positive about each new day!

*You will need: Access to some Foxgloves in the wild, a pen, some paper, and a handful of bread crumbs.*

- Sit before a clump of these blooms. Admire their beauty, notice how they make you feel.
- Think about how you'd like to feel, for example, happy or energized.
- Write this down in the form of a wish, such as "I wish to be happy and excited for each new day."
- Leave the paper near the Foxgloves, and as an offering to the fairies and birds, scatter the bread crumbs nearby.

# PHLOX

*Phlox*

Phlox is a herbaceous bloom with
tubular flowers, usually blue, pink,
or purple. They have flaring petals
and slender leaves.

**FLOWER MEANING** Associated
with unity, companionship, uplifting
energy, and harmony.

**FOLKLORE ORIGIN** India/America

## THE LOST CLOUD

Where the misty mountains and verdant valleys flow,
and the forests cluster at their feet, a flower blooms en
masse. Appearing when the light returns to drink in
the freshness of spring, its dense fluffy blooms merge
from palest sky blue, to sweet magenta. Carpeting
the woodland in softness, the flower known as Phlox
comes in many forms. But in this, its purest state, it
tells a story of companionship, of nature working in
harmony to create a colorful miracle.

Once upon a time, the Phlox had no color at all.
Like tiny, feathered clouds of whiteness, it bathed
the land in a blanket of calm. To the native tribes
it was both soothing and uplifting, a herald of the
warmer season, and a sign to plant, nurture, and
work the land. But while the Phlox was pleased to
bring joy to the hearts of humans, it longed to be
as pretty and vibrant as some of the other flowers.
Even so, it enjoyed its place in the cycle of life, and

was content to be a spring bloom. And while the Phlox unleashed its beauty for all the world to see, above in the sky, the clouds were also having their moment.

As bright as snow, with puffed up chests that billowed as they sailed, they came in many sizes. There were streaks of willowy softness, followed by a parade of shorter splodges. Heavy with rain, but warm from the sun, they floated through the ether. Sometimes it seemed they disappeared from sight completely, only to reemerge under the sun's rays. The clouds, like the Phlox, were a reminder of the changing seasons, and their shifting shapes were a delight for those who had the time to stop and stare.

But the clouds needed rest too. Carrying all of that rain and appearing as light as a feather is quite a feat and takes energy, so at night when the sun would retreat from the heavens and the world was cast into darkness, they would seek refuge at the top of the mountains. They would settle and meld into the peaks, and drift into a dreamless sleep, only to be reborn in the morning. Each cloud had its favorite spot, hidden by the mists and snowfall, and it would make its way there under the moon's watchful eye. But there was one little cloud who had only recently formed. A tender bundle of joy, he would drift through the sky, taking in the view below. In particular, he loved to look at the flowers, and often wondered what it would feel like to wrap his vaporous fingers around their delicate petals.

One day, as the sun began to make its steady journey over the horizon, the little cloud found himself completely alone. He wasn't sure how it had happened. He'd been trailing behind a streak of dancing clouds much bigger than himself, but instead of trying to keep up, he'd become lost in thought. It was easy to do that when you were cloud, for there was nothing much else to do but daydream. And so, he'd been left behind.

While all the others had shuffled off to bed, the little cloud was left hanging in the darkness. He shivered and tried to stretch out as thin as he could, to go unnoticed, but the night was a strange place and he felt afraid. And so he drifted down to earth, in search of a mountain he could make his own. Try as he might, he could not find a safe resting place. It seemed that all the peaks had vanished in the shadows, and so the tiny cloud turned his attention to the earth and that's when he saw the Phlox and his heart leapt with joy.

The starry blooms were gazing upward, trying to attract his attention. With open fronds and warm moist roots, they offered him a place to rest, a sanctuary from the gloom. He fell to the ground, so relieved to find a safe spot he began to cry. His tears glistened, causing his ethereal form to shift from white, to gentle pink, and lavender, and slowly, gracefully, he drifted into the deepest slumber. His body spread upon the flat earth and soaked into the friendly flowers, and they were only too glad to receive him. Together these unusual bedfellows slept under a blanket of stars, until the morning came.

As the sun peeped over the mountains, the little cloud began to rise, his malleable form stretching to fill the space. It seemed that overnight he had gained strength and substance and was ready to take his place with the others in his tribe. But he wasn't the only one who had changed, for the Phlox that had drunk his tears of gratitude was also transformed. With open petals now stained by the cloud's pearlescent hues, the flower at last had color. The Phlox was exuberant and thankful for this gift. In being selfless, and uniting with the cloud, it had allowed its natural beauty to shine. From that day onward its pretty flowers would be likened to evening clouds floating over the meadows—warm, yielding, and forever uplifting.

## RITUAL TO HELP YOU GROW AND FLOURISH

Tending to flowers in the yard is a nurturing exercise which can also help you grow. To carry out this ritual, you will need to plant some Phlox plants.

*You will need: A yard, border or planter, some Phlox plants, a trowel, water, secateurs and, time to tend to them.*

- Choose a sunny spot as this flower enjoys light, warmth, and moist soil. If you have more than one shrub, plant them at least sixty centimeters apart. Water well and ensure that they're continually hydrated through the summer.
- Deadhead your Phlox regularly. As you snip away the waning flowerheads, consider the things in your own life that you need to release in order for you to breathe, and flourish.
- Imagine giving yourself a prune, and cutting away negative beliefs and behavior patterns that hold you back.
- At the end of the flowering season, separate any large leggy clumps to allow the roots of the plant to spread and receive an abundance of nutrients. Do this by digging up at the roots and gently splitting the plant into three smaller shrubs.
- As you do this, consider how you might allow yourself to grow. What would give you room to breathe, and allow you to step out of your comfort zone?
- Think of three positive steps you could take to help you blossom.
- Finally, replant the newly separated shrubs, leaving space between them so that they have room to breathe.

# Chapter 4
# WINTER

## EARLY BLOOMERS

Winter may have cast its snowy cloak upon the ground, but the flowers within this section are not so easily deterred. Their tenacity to bloom, to find a way beneath the solid soil, and seek the solace of the sky, is what carries them forward. Frost may nip at each tender tendril but it cannot sway them from the cause, for these are the pioneers of the plant world, the ground-breaking trailblazers who were born to herald the coming of spring. From delicate fluted lovelies the color of snow, to the dancing Bluebells that carpet the woodland in the deepest indigo hue, these are the blooms that make you stop in your tracks and behold their beauty. And their stories are just as mesmerizing. For while they may appear fragile at first glance these flowers are deceptively strong and have the power to transport you to other worlds, and new heights of understanding.

# ACONITE
## *Aconitum napellus*

Aconite is a herbaceous perennial with hairless stems and rounded leaves. The flowers are helmet shaped and usually vibrant blue or purple.

**FLOWER MEANING** Associated with death, the underworld, rebirth, and balance.

**FOLKLORE ORIGIN** India

## SHIVA'S POTION

At the dawn of time, when the Hindu gods were in residence upon the tumbling rock that was the Earth, there was one among them known as the Auspicious One. With skin as pale as bone dust, and dark eyes that seemed to tell the story of the Universe, he shone from within, and his name was Shiva. For many his light was confusing, for he was both Destroyer and Restorer, and two sides of the same coin. That said, he had a huge following, those who wanted to learn and benefit from his teachings, and those who were in awe of his greatness. After all he was a magnificent sight, with the river Ganges streaming from the tip of his skull (a nod to his extensive knowledge which flowed freely to the masses) and a third eye in the center of his forehead to represent inner wisdom. Then there was the tiger skin slung loose about his shoulders, to show that he controlled his animalistic instincts.

Shiva was a conundrum, but he was a benevolent deity who cared deeply about his people. Most of all he took his dual role as a herdsman of souls, and wrathful avenger, seriously, and would do anything to restore the balance of good and evil.

At this time, the gods, or Devas as they were known in their collective group, began to crave the elixir of immortality known as the Amrit. It seemed only fitting that they should be given this gift so that they could remain in the heavens forever. Shiva, as one of the most prominent among them, agreed. But after much discussion it became apparent that it would not be an easy task. They must churn the primordial Ocean of Milk, a feat that even the Devas in their entirety could not achieve. They would need the assistance of the Demons they had been fighting since the beginning of the Universe, and they would have to work in harmony, taking their turn at the ocean center to achieve their goal.

After much discussion an agreement was made between the two sides. The Demons would be given half of the potion as a reward for their assistance. But as with all things cosmic and magical, it was not simply a case of stirring the pot. The ocean was vast and timeless, a milky sea of clouds which stretched as far as the eye could see. Not only that, it was thick like molten lead, and impossible to move. The Devas realized that the stirring of this life force could take millions of years, so they agreed to work as a team, each one offering up some of their time for the cause.

They used Mount Mandara as a churning rod and the snake king Vasuki as the rope, but it still took an age. Their efforts revealed little of the Amrit at first, but the Devas and the Demons did not give up, and eventually the milky seas brought forth the Amrit and many other gifts, as they'd expected.

Being such a primal sludge, there were other things that lurked within the depths of this ocean, things that should never see the light of day. One such offering was the *Hala Hala*, the essence of all the poisons in the world which swirled to the top, leaving a dark stain upon the sea's surface. The gods who were present reeled in horror. They did not know what to do. How should they deal with this noxious potion? Would it prove fatal if it were unleashed? In terror they ran to Mount Kailash where Shiva sat meditating and asked his advice.

The god was only too happy to help. He had no fear of the poison, for he was accustomed to both the light and dark, and held both in his hands. And so with careful precision he extracted the liquid and drank the hideous potion to spare the rest of the world from its venomous fumes. Whether it would have killed him had he been left to his own devices, we will never know, for his wife Parvati was not prepared to take that chance. She grasped his throat within her hands and choked him so that the poison would remain trapped there for eternity. The lethal concoction tainted his skin, and his throat turned blue as it settled within.

Shiva had saved the world with this one selfless act; however, a few tiny drops of the toxic potion had trickled onto his fingers and fell to earth in small droplets, which seeped beneath the soil. These little beads formed buds, which bloomed into beautiful blue flowers, and the remaining poison surged through the roots and stem of the plant known as Aconite.

The pretty flower soon became a reminder of Shiva's power and generosity of spirit, but it was also a symbol of death, the underworld, and the shadier parts of the soul. As it grew and flourished around the world, it became a herald of spring and of new beginnings, but in its darker guise it was a call to arms, urging those who picked its sweet blooms to embrace both sides of their personality, and like Shiva, to seek balance in all things.

## RITUAL TO PROMOTE A SENSE OF BALANCE AND WHOLENESS

Aconite has a number of names, from Thor's Hat, to Wolfsbane, and a myriad of different interpretations. While it's seen as a symbol of hope and rebirth, it also has a dark side, making it the perfect flower to work with when you need some balance.

*You will need: A piece of paper, and a pen.*

- Take the paper, and draw a giant circle in the center. This represents you as a whole.
- Draw a line down the middle of the circle to split it into two halves.
- On one half write down any negative traits that spring to mind when you think about your personality, for example you might think you are "irritable" or "impatient."
- On the flip side of the circle, write the opposite trait, so you might say "easygoing" or "patient."
- Once you have a list of positive words, draw some petals around the circle to represent the Aconite flower.
- Within each petal write one thing you could do to embrace the positive aspect you have outlined—so if you want to be more "easygoing" you might decide to meditate or implement a breathing exercise into your daily routine to calm your mind.
- When you have completed the flower, place it somewhere that you'll see it every day as a reminder to balance the darker and lighter aspects of your personality.

# VIOLET
## *Viola*

Violets are a herbaceous perennial with a sweet scent. Their nodding blooms have five petals, which are usually blue to purple in shade.

**FLOWER MEANING** Associated with faith, honesty, spiritual wisdom, and innocence.

**FOLKLORE ORIGIN** Greece

## THE MOST BEAUTIFUL WOMAN IN THE WORLD

In the beginning of time, when the Earth was a mix of land and sea and nothing much else, the gods were created. Formed from the cosmos, each one had a role to play in shaping the world as it is today. There were powerful deities who controlled the elements, and those who crafted the landscape. There were the ones responsible for the rising sun and the shifting moon, and those who governed everything in between, but while it seemed there was a god for everything, something was missing from the pantheon. Love, and all the emotions associated with it, did not exist. And so it was no surprise that when the Titan Cronus cast his father's genitals into the sea, Venus as she was known to the Romans, was born from his seed and became the goddess of love and beauty.

The epitome of love, she was a stunning creation, emerging from the depths of the ocean in a giant scallop shell. An alluring goddess, it seemed that she was there to tempt both gods and men, and this she did with great aplomb. Venus was not known for her coyness, quite the opposite—she radiated confidence and knew the power of her gorgeousness. In fact, she reveled in it. Some might say she was conceited, and others self-assured, but it mattered little to her, as long as they thought she was the most beautiful woman in the world.

One day the goddess was having a heated debate with her son Cupid. It started innocently as a discussion over the power of love and how it could make the ugliest of fools appear desirable, then swiftly escalated into a contest of one-upmanship. Venus liked to win at everything and there was nothing she loved more, apart from love itself, than a good argument. Cupid, being the god of love and keeper of the arrow, believed that everyone deserved romance. They could be tall, short, fat, thin, their looks mattered less than what was in their heart, but Venus, being full of vanity, disagreed.

"The outer appearance, reflects the inner," she argued, and then pointed to a group of young girls who were playing in a fountain below them. "See, how sweet and innocent they are, and how pretty they look."

"I don't disagree, they are indeed innocent and very beautiful," said Cupid, smiling to himself. He had chosen his words carefully, in the hope that they would strike a chord with the goddess. In truth, he was annoyed with his mother. Her haughty manner and the way she held herself was starting to irritate the god, and although he was cherub-like in appearance, he was far from angelic in his ways.

"Beautiful?" she spat. "I wouldn't say that."

"Do you not think so?" he smirked. "I would go as far to say, that they are *the most* beautiful girls in the world."

Venus frowned. "More beautiful than me?"

Cupid laughed. "Oh Mother, really? Do you want me to answer that?"

The goddess wavered for a moment, her lip trembling. "They can't be more beautiful than me, I am the goddess of love and beauty! Tell me! Are they more beautiful than me?"

Cupid shrugged. "Well they have youth on their side, so yes, I think so."

The goddess was enraged. How could the girls be better than her, it was impossible. *She was the most beautiful woman in the world*, and yet if it was so, then she needed to do something about it. There was only room for one goddess of love.

Sweeping all other humans aside, she burst through the ether taking the young girls by surprise. They immediately fell to their knees, but this mark of respect failed to impress her. Venus was consumed with anger. It poured through her veins like poison. The earth shuddered at the force of her fury, and the girls threw themselves at her mercy, but it was of no use. The goddess grew in size and stature, the rage consumed her taking away any reason, or kindness. She stretched out her hands, pointing them at the cowering group beneath her, and in an instant they turned to dirt. The youthful beauty that had fuelled her jealousy was now a distant memory, replaced by grains of soil that lay in clumps at her feet. "What have you done?" cried Cupid. Even he had not imagined she would go this far.

She shook her head, dazed, and confused by the power of her wrath, then she gazed at the mounds she had created. It seemed that something was happening, the air which had been thick with rage, now shimmered before her and slowly. The earth began to transform. The surface began to splinter forming cracks that revealed roots and thick stems. Upon these youthful tendrils heads appeared, many petaled and the deepest lavender blue. Leaves gathered in heart shaped clusters, as the delicate blooms unleashed their glory. Where the girls had once clutched each other in terror now a patch of Violets grew in abundance, at last safe and able to unleash their loveliness without fear. Vivacious and vibrant, they shone in the morning sun, and those that saw them would agree, that in that moment, they were more beautiful than any other flower upon the Earth.

Venus remained silent for a minute, and then reclaiming her composure, she turned to Cupid and flashed him a wide smile.

"See, I told you *I* was the most beautiful woman in the world."

---

## RITUAL TO CONNECT WITH YOUR INNER WISDOM

Often used to treat skin conditions like eczema, Violets are anti-inflammatory and can be used as a tonic to cleanse the blood. Their purple hue makes them synonymous with wisdom and intuition.

*You will need: A place to sit down, some time and space to connect with your intuition.*

- Start by finding a comfortable space to sit, where you won't be disturbed. Relax and focus on your breathing.
- When you inhale, imagine that you're breathing in a violet color.
- Picture yourself covered from head to toe in the vibrant hue. See it washing over your body, traveling along your spine and into the center of your chest.
- See the color behind your eyes and let it soothe your mind.
- As you exhale, imagine releasing a wave of violet energy which sweeps over everything.
- Continue to cocoon yourself in this color as you breathe, and notice how this makes you feel.
- After a couple of minutes, open your mind and let any thoughts flow into your head.
- Make a note of anything that feels significant as it could be a message from your intuitive self.

# SNOWDROP
## *Galanthus nivalis*

Snowdrop is a tender perennial with white bell-shaped flowers composed of six tepals upon a short erect stem. The leaves are smooth and linear.

**FLOWER MEANING** Associated with purity, hope, and rebirth.

**FOLKLORE ORIGIN** Germany

## THE COLOR OF SNOW

At the beginning of time, when the world was nothing but a blank space and a colorless vista, there existed the elements. Wild and free, they roamed the Earth with the power to create and shape at will.

The wind was seamless, a thin sooty veil, that swept through the land scattering a gray dust over everything. The rain, which dropped from the sky in sheets of silver to form inky blue rivers, was perhaps the most colorful of them all, and soon evolved its own way of being. The sunshine, a product of the fiery orb that was the sun, couldn't help but develop a golden shimmer, and slowly and surely, the combination of water and heat and wind gusts to spread the seeds, made the plants and flowers grow. Saplings became trees, and the muddy earth gave way to a carpet of the softest green. An abundance of flowers sprang forth, their rainbow shades sparkling like jewels amid the undergrowth.

At last the planet was coming to life, each tiny piece of nature adding depth and texture to the

colorful canvas. But there was still one element that had failed to find a shade for itself. Cold and alone, it trudged soberly through hills and valleys leaving a pallid sludge behind, and the longer it searched for a hue to match its true nature the more disheartened and drab it became. Eventually the element, called Snow, decided it needed some assistance. Seeking refuge in a woodland meadow, it sank into the grass and with a heavy sigh said, "Please, help," to whoever might listen.

The trees and flowers shuffled closer to this pale ghost, and whispered "What do you want us to do?"

Snow, weak from his travels, muttered, "I need a color of my own. Would any of you give me your hue?"

This caused a commotion among the gathered flora.

"Give up our colors! We can't do that!"

"I am known for my indigo glow," said the tiny Lavender. "I could not give it up!"

"And my emerald green is a part of who I am," cried the Grass.

"My crimson petals are what make me special!" yelled the Poppy.

"Me too!" chimed the red Rose.

And so it went on, and poor Snow became downcast. Tiny rivulets of tears smeared his face, and he sank further into the ground. There was nothing he could do. He couldn't force the flowers to give up their hues for him. He couldn't steal their tints away in the night, for that was when they hid their beautiful faces. He sat, and he sagged under the weight of his own futility, and just when he thought that his days as an element were done, a tiny, delicate flower stepped forward and reached out a leafy frond.

"You can have my color," said the Snowdrop in a small voice. "I will gladly give it, if it helps."

Snow, who was slowly beginning to melt, sat up and looked at the drooping tubular bloom. Such a pretty little flower and so selfless. The offer was beyond kind, and it instantly restored hope within his icy heart.

"You would sacrifice your color just for me?"

The Snowdrop quivered, "If it would make you happy, sir."

Slowly and steadily, Snow began to retain form and shape, pulling himself back from the landscape.

"What an honor," he said. "Your kindness has given me an idea! Why don't we share the color? You and I both could use it, and it will be a way of recognizing each other."

The Snowdrop nodded in the breeze.

"And to show my gratitude little flower, I will let you bloom at the end of winter, and you will be protected from the snow that I bring, and the frosty mornings that I leave behind. You will thrive in the cold air, and the ice that accompanies my showers will never dull your petals."

Snow paused. "And because you have restored the hope in my heart, you will be forever associated with new beginnings, and the coming of spring. We will be siblings, sharing the purest white hue, and our name will be recognized by all humans, and they will smile when they see us."

The Snowdrop swayed with joy, "How can I thank you for this honor?"

But Snow was already gone, climbing the hill with a renewed vigour to his gait. His newly found color had settled about his shoulders, and it suited him well. The gleaming whiteness sparkled in the last rays of the day's sunshine, and it looked more resplendent than any of the rainbow shades. The other flowers watched him go, and while they were glad to feel the cool weight of his personality lift from the land, they also looked on with regret. If only they had been as generous as little Snowdrop, they too might have become the herald of spring. As it was, they would always follow Snowdrop's gentle footsteps into each new year.

And so the world was finally ready for human kind. All of the elements had colors, which they wore with pride, and the environment was awash with color. And as promised, the Snowdrop blossomed each year at the end of winter, appearing in fine clumps—an unassuming white bloom, and a symbol of hope, love, and new beginnings.

## RITUAL TO CLEANSE THE MIND AND INSPIRE HOPE

Snowdrops are easily identifiable, thanks to the purity of their white bell-shaped blooms. This ritual cleansing white hue to help you connect with the flower and feel renewed.

*You will need: Space to sit, and a large white scarf or piece of material.*

- Sit and take a minute to adjust your posture, roll your shoulders back, and lengthen your spine.
- Wrap the scarf around your shoulders and close your eyes. Take a deep breath in and imagine you're drawing in the pure white energy of the Snowdrop. Feel it permeate your being.
- As you exhale, imagine this energy traveling around your body. It filters through every muscle and sinew, filling you with optimism and clearing away any negative energy.
- Continue to breathe in this way, visualizing the white light flooding your system.
- Think of what the Snowdrop means to you, and think of word which sums up this quality, for example "hope" or "rebirth."
- As you inhale the white energy, imagine it is infused with this quality and say the word in your mind.
- Repeat this breathing cycle for a couple of minutes, then relax and give your body a shake.

# PROTEA

*Protea cynaroides*

Protea has a thick sturdy stem and large leaves, which are hairy at first, but become smooth as they mature. Its flowerheads are surrounded with layers of colorful bracts.

FLOWER MEANING Associated with with courage, resilience, and transformation.

FOLKLORE ORIGIN Africa

## THE PETALED PHOENIX

Hundreds of millions of years before the first dinosaur reared its head, a species of flower existed. At first just a tiny frond that pushed through the cracks in the barren soil, it was hard to tell exactly what it was. In truth, it must have appeared alien as it grew into a fleshy stem, with a twisting taproot. Devoid of color or pattern, it yearned for the light and warmth of the sun, and this it got unreservedly.

The fiery orb unleashed its blaze, burning the surface of the planet, and answering the shrub's prayers. Slowly over time it began to grow, taking shape and form. Its stem thickened, and its leaves became large and hairy in the first flush of youth. Soon the flowerheads would emerge surrounded by colorful bracts, each one enormous and woolly in appearance, a match for any mammoth. And so the Protea was born. And for the longest time it lived in almost isolation, being King of the Flowers—a title that went unchallenged.

It was inevitable that as the climate shifted, other blooms would start sprouting from the earth. Some were hardy, colorless, blending in with the dusty environment, and most had adapted and learned how to harness the elements. Bare stalks soon became tall, reedy stems, framed by a halo of leaves, each one producing an array of buds, and then came the pretty petaled heads that burst with colorful potential. And so the Protea was not on its own anymore. It was one of many different flower species, all vying for attention.

From large vibrant rainbow hues to intricately patterned leaves, symmetrically arranged for viewing pleasure. The air was enriched with a blend of scents, from citrus sweet to mellow vanilla and everything in between. Each bloom had its merits, and they were all contenders for the crown. The Protea, having been there first, protested its magnificence in color and stature, claiming this alone should make it the King of Flowers, but the others disagreed. They had a heated discussion on the subject, each believing that they had a right to the throne.

They squabbled for days, unable to come to any agreement. The other creatures watched in amusement at first, but after a while they joined in the argument. The birds who fed upon the seeds twittered and sang about the flowers they liked the best. The bees that drank the nectar flapped, and danced, and spoke of the blooms that had the sweetest gifts. The beetles that took shelter beneath the greenery championed the leafier contenders, and the other creatures who often fed upon their foliage voted with hungry mouths. It seemed that everyone had an opinion, which differed greatly. The flowers reached an uncomfortable impasse, and it would have stayed that way, had it not been for the sun, who had been watching the commotion impatiently.

Turning up his brightness with ferocious glee, the shining orb began to burn, knowing this would sort the wheat from the chaff. On and on it blazed until the ground beneath sweltered. The plants began to wither under the sun's scorching rays. The earth began to blister, the brittle surface splintering. Most of the vegetation curled inward, retreating from the intense heat. It could not withstand the onslaught and eventually died. A few plants clung on, gasping for any tendril of cool air that they could drink and any hint of moisture that might sustain them, but the sun was undeterred—if there was going to be a King of Flowers it would surely be the one that could survive anything. And so it seared the earth with a last fortifying blast of fire, which spread through the trees and roots, through the grasses and leaves and the remaining flowers. It hit the tips of the mountains where the Protea stood proudly, burning through the surface leaving a smoky trail of destruction. Once more the planet was a wasteland with nothing to show of the life that had once been there.

The sun let out a breath, and calmly dimmed its light. It disappeared from the horizon, content that at least now it would be left in peace. But it had not counted on the survival of the Protea. After all, this was the first and most important flower, and unlike all of the others, it had a thick underground stem made for such occasions. Covered in tiny dormant buds beneath the surface, it was like the mythical phoenix and able to regenerate after death. Its lifeless appearance was a guise, a way for the bloom to protect itself and survive fire and flood. Not only that, it was strong in other ways, able to shapeshift and withstand the changing climate. And so in a short time it grew again, standing tall and proud, with a parade of vivid flowerheads. It flourished upon stony, brittle ground, in poor soil and at high altitude, thriving in the savage heat and shifting temperatures.

And when the other flowers eventually returned, they too had to agree that the Protea had proved its worth and was the rightful King of Flowers. It had remained stoic and true, facing the elements with courage, and returning from the dead to claim its prize. That is how the mighty Protea became known by the people of the land—as a survivor, a fighter, and the petaled phoenix of the flower kingdom.

## RITUAL TO PROMOTE CREATIVITY

Use this many layered, colorful bloom as inspiration, by taking a moment of stillness to appreciate its beauty.

*You will need: An image of a Protea in full bloom, or the real thing, a piece of paper, a pen, colored pencils, and any other crafty tools you feel drawn to.*

- Spend a few minutes sitting quietly in the company of the flower, whether you're gazing at an image, or you have the real thing. Consider the way it looks. Is there anything that stands out, for example, any notable markings or patterns?
- Consider how it makes you feel. What words spring to mind as you gaze at its form?
- Write down your instinctive response and circle any key words or emotions that resonate with you.
- Now let your imagination take over. You might want to have a go at describing the flower in poetic form or drawing the bloom. You could create a collage of colors and shapes that represent what the flower means to you. Whatever you decide to do, this is your creation, and it doesn't have to be perfect.

# RAGWORT
## *Jacobaea vulgaris*

Ragwort is a biennial or perennial herb with tall, strong stems, and large flat-topped clusters of bright yellow flowers.

**FLOWER MEANING** Associated with protection and safety.

**FOLKLORE ORIGIN** Ireland

## THE FAIRY CHARIOT

Fairies may have wings, but these dazzling beauties are mostly for show. If you look at them in detail, you will notice they are paper thin, and will turn to dust at the slightest touch. It is not common knowledge among human folk, but that's because the wee folk keep themselves to themselves.

Should a human capture a fairy, then all of their secrets will be gone and the mystery of the fey will be a thing of past. This makes them super protective, and canny in the ways of the world. That's not to say that they don't interact with the environment. Fairies love nature, for it serves them in many ways. Since medieval times, the fey have been at one with the earth, and every creature upon it. They have danced among the tall grasses, slept beneath the shade of the Hawthorn tree, flown upon sparrow's wings, and ridden on the back of field mice. Fairies are adept at subterfuge, and they know that humans are mostly

full of their own concerns, and hardly likely to notice what is under their noses. But it wasn't always this way. In the Middle Ages the belief in fairies was rife, making it virtually impossible if they wished to migrate from foreign shores. The wee folk needed a way of reaching their brothers and sisters in the greener isles without being noticed, but how do you travel so far when your wings are gossamer thin? Sprites aren't built for arduous tasks, making long journeys impractical.

And so the fairy courts of Europe met, and with the magical assistance of their feline friends, communed with those of the emerald isle known as Ireland, where their relatives resided. Gazing into the eyes of the cat, they summoned their cousins across the pond, who they could see through the window of the iris and discussed their options.

"We could ride on the back of rats in the hope that they might board ships to bring us to your isle!"

"We could ask the witches; they might have a spell we could use?"

"We could hide in luggage, and hope that the humans don't spot us?"

And so it went on. Each idea had its faults, whether that was being eaten as a rat's supper, or being discovered by humans.

In the end, it was a small flower fairy who stepped forward and offered an alternative.

"What about using flowers? They are always being transported overseas. We could hide among the petals, and no one would see us if we choose the right bloom."

A wave of silence passed through the gathered fey as they pondered the suggestion, and it was quickly agreed that this was the most feasible option. But which flower to pick?

There were some who argued for the Rose, a popular bloom, and a favorite with humans. While it came in many sizes to accommodate a range of fairy beings, it was riddled with prickly thorns, and often admired, meaning it would be easy to spot a sprite whilst under scrutiny. Daffodils were also cited, but being a spring bloom it meant that travel would be limited to early in the year, and that simply wouldn't meet the demands of the more adventurous fey. Bluebells suffered the same fate, and being delicate flowers, there wasn't much to obscure the larger fairies with bigger wings. Tulips were another suggestion. Their cupped blooms made great hidey-holes, but they were rather troublesome to escape, having high-sided petals. It was decided that this too would not work.

On and on it went, with flowers discarded for size, shape, color, scent, and when they were likely to blossom. In the end it seemed that no bloom could do the job perfectly.

It was then that the lowly Ragwort, affectionately known as "Stinking Willie," stepped forward, having listened to all of the discussion.

"If I may be so bold," the sturdy stemmed flower said, "I am the ideal choice to carry you wherever you need to go. My stem is stout but long, and I bear more than one flower. I carry many clusters of the brightest yellow blooms upon my shoulders which provide a safe space for you to rest. Not only that, but I spread easily, and I am hard to get rid of. I can transport you and give you a safe haven when you need to rest, but I am unlikely to be noticed by humankind, who cannot stand the smell of my leaves and tend to think of me as a weed."

The fairies carefully considered all of the points the flower had presented, and they realized that they could not argue with any of the Ragwort's reasoning.

From that day forward, the golden wildflower with its vibrant clusters and wretched smelling leaves became the preferred mode of transport and a chariot for the fey. They were safe and comfortable among the blooms and hidden from prying eyes. The smell, though off-putting, meant that most animals and humans gave it a wide berth, and the fairies were able to ride to and from Ireland to visit their kin. Not only that, but they could preserve their fragile wings and keep them in top condition, should they ever be required to have them on show.

## RITUAL TO FEEL SAFE AND PROTECTED IN NATURE

A wide range of insects rely on Ragwort for nourishment. Being the sole source of sustenance to thirty different species, this plant has become a staple of the countryside, and a place where many take shelter.

*You will need: Somewhere outside that you can sit undisturbed in nature, and a blanket (optional).*

- Find a meadow, field, or patch of grass where you can lay in comfort.
- If you have a blanket with you, lay it down, and sit with your legs out in front of you.
- Slowly lower your back until you are laying down. Take your time and ease each vertebrae into the ground.
- Breathe deeply as you do this and relax your muscles. Let your limbs grow heavy.
- Notice how the earth feels beneath you, how it supports you and offers a firm foundation.
- Imagine that you are reclining among a patch of Ragwort. Bring the image to mind in your head and feel the comfort of being surrounded by these pretty blooms.
- Here among these wildflowers you are obscured from the world, protected, and able to fully relax and be yourself.
- Let any thoughts come and go and enjoy the natural sanctuary that you have created with your mind.

# VALERIAN
## *Valeriana officinalis*

Valerian is a clumping perennial
with sparsely-leaved stems. The
leaves are dark green and toothed.
The delicate flowers are white or
pale pink.

**FLOWER MEANING** Associated
with strength, charisma, vitality, and
personal power.

**FOLKLORE ORIGIN** Germany

### THE PIPER'S CHARM

It started with a handful of rats seen scampering
through the streets. They had matted fur and slender
snouted noses to sniff out trouble and tasty titbits.
It wasn't that unusual, especially in a town which
thrived on industry. From butchers to bakers and
those who sold their wares on the streets, there were
plenty of scraps, so pests were expected. The people
weren't enamored, but they paid little attention to the
furry invaders.

Within a couple of days the numbers had grown.
The rats were doing what rats did best and multiplying
at such a rate that soon it became commonplace to
see the long-tailed trespassers scurrying over the
cobbles toward the market or gathering in groups
in alleyways. It seemed they were gaining force and
forming armies of warm bodies, and nothing could
deter them. Not fire or water, or stones hurled in
their direction, and definitely not insults or spells, of

which there were a few. As the days rolled on, the problem escalated. There were rats everywhere.

To onlookers who passed the city gates, it seemed that the town was heaving beneath the onslaught. From crawling walls, to wriggling drainpipes, wherever you looked you'd find a battalion of bright-eyed creatures ready to pounce.

The mayor was beside himself; he had appealed to all four corners of the land for assistance with his problem, but help was thin on the ground. Then one day a handsome young man wearing an outfit of many colors knocked upon his door.

"I can help with your problem if you pay me well. I will banish the rats and send them to hell!"

The mayor was intrigued by this poetic stranger and said yes immediately, for he was prepared to try anything. The man smiled and bowed and shook his hand, and then produced a crude looking pipe from pocket.

"Tell the townsfolk to stay inside, lock their doors, away and hide."

That morning after a deal between the piper and the mayor had been struck, a warning was issued that everyone should remain in their homes so that the piper could work his magic, and this he did with such charm and eloquence, for he was a minstrel and clever too. He knew that the secret was to lure the rats away with a scent that would tickle their senses and he had just the thing—a pretty wildflower by the name of Valerian. With delicate pink blooms and a pungent aroma, it would do the trick and do it well, for the smell was not just appealing to animals, but any creature pure of heart, and youthful. He stuffed his pockets with the flowering herb and danced through the streets playing a soulful tune, and the rats began to follow. They trailed his every move, darting from their nests at the speed of light, for they couldn't get enough of the enticing aroma. The piper skipped and hopped and weaved through the cobbleways, until all of the rats were in his thrall. Then he led them out of the town, along dusty roads, over the hills and to the top of a cliff, where they all fell to their doom.

The mayor was thrilled. He had no idea what magic the piper had used to eliminate the rats, but it mattered not. The town of Hamelin was restored to its former glory, and all was well. Except that the mayor was a greedy man, and a miser at heart and he didn't like parting with money, so when the piper came to collect his reward, he offered him half of what he'd promised.

"The deal was made, the debt still stands, what happens now is in your hands," said the mercurial piper.

Performing a graceful pirouette, he made his way out onto the bustling streets, and pulling a fresh bundle of Valerian from his bag, he stuffed his pockets to the brim. The scent was intoxicating for those of a gentle persuasion. Lifting his pipe to his lips, he began to play a haunting melody. At first it seemed that no one noticed, but then slowly, steadily, a stream of children began to follow in his footsteps. They meandered along, their wide eyes twinkling as they inhaled the flower's fragrance. Soon the straddlers became a crowd, and the children began to run, to leap from their beds and burst from their homes, and to fall over each other to get closer to the piper.

The townsfolk watched in horror as the piper began to lead the children away, and it didn't matter how much they yelled, or tried to drag their children to safety, they couldn't stop them. It was as if their babies were possessed, imbued with supernatural strength, thanks to the piper's charm.

On and on he danced, and the children danced with him. Where they went, no one knows. Whether they suffered a similar fate to the rats or the piper let them go remains a mystery, but the town of Hamelin was never the same again thanks to the enigmatic piper and the alluring wildflower in his pocket.

## RITUAL TO HARVEST AND NURTURE NEW GROWTH, AND CONNECT WITH NATURE

Valerian grows in abundance in abandoned areas and favors moist shady spaces. This lovely wildflower is best foraged between June and August, when you're likely to see the flowers in full bloom. Replanting this bloom can help you nurture new growth.

*You will need: A notebook, a pen, and a pair of secateurs (optional).*

- Go for a walk along the edges of the woods or by a river bank on a sunny day.
- Keep a notebook and pen at your side, so that you can note down if you spot any Valerian growing in the wild and where it is located.
- Take your time, and engage your senses as you walk, but pay particular attention to any shady spots that have been left untended.
- Look for five-petaled blooms that are white or pale pink and leaves which give off a pungent aroma similar to that of stinky cheese or sweaty feet.
- If you're looking to harvest a plant for your own yard, then cut the stems near the base of the plant and lift the roots gently from the soil. These should be white, stringy and a good length.
- Replant the roots of the plant in a shady spot, and water well to encourage new growth.

# BELLFLOWER
## *Campanula*

Bellflower is a herbaceous perennial with delicate blue nodding flowers that are bell-shaped and have short lobes.

**FOLKLORE MEANING** Associated with gratitude, everlasting love, enchantment, and beauty.

**FOLKLORE ORIGIN** Greece

## THE MAGIC MIRROR

Since the beginning of time the humble mirror has been a symbol of magical significance. It may be a simple tool to capture the reflection, but the essence held within resonates from the surface. Depending on the type of mirror, it shifts and changes, reflecting the querant's hopes and dreams at that moment. Whether used to primp and preen, or for more esoteric concerns like divining the future, or connecting with the spirits of lost loved ones, mirrors exude mystery, which makes them prized among gods and mortals.

So imagine a very special mirror, blessed by the Roman goddess of love and beauty, Venus: a glittering handheld spectacle, with an intricately carved frame. Picture the gleam of enchantment that sparkles when you gaze upon the surface, the power that emanates from within, and how it might affect those who happen upon its splendor. Such was the fate of a young shepherd boy, who was wandering

the stony cliffs in search of errant sheep when he stumbled across the mirror wedged between a slice of rock. How it got there is anyone's guess. For while it was usually in Venus's possession, she was known for her flights of fancy, and her lusty ways could make her careless.

The boy was immediately taken with the object. He had never seen a mirror before and was not accustomed to the shape and form of his own face, having only glimpsed a hint of its beauty while bathing in the stream. He picked it up, and gazed freely at himself, and as he did he felt something change within. Some might say a switch was flicked in his chest, a tiny trigger which allowed love to flow. As the boy's lips curled into a wide grin, he could feel the energy growing, the warmth flooding his body. His skin, tanned and ruddy from working outside, seemed to shimmer as if lit by the morning sun. His eyes shone like the Aegean Ocean, their sapphire depths rippling with secrets, and his smile grew more confident with every second. He was in love with his reflection and transfixed by this new possession. Not only that, he felt gratitude for the first time, for he was thankful of this gift and joyful to be alive.

Venus, who had witnessed the boy's transformation from her seat in the stars, was not happy. After all, it was *her* enchanted mirror. It didn't matter that she had lost it in the first place, that was irrelevant. The youth must be parted from his treasure, and soon.

Being a goddess, you would think this would be an easy task, but even with her immense will and mystical gifts, the boy could not be swayed. She tried inflicting her thoughts upon him, manipulating him with sweet words and promises of future greatness, but her whispers fell on deaf ears. The boy was so taken with the mirror and the joy it gave him that he would not let it go. Instead he clung tighter to the ornate handle, making it a part of him.

She tried forcing the elements to steal the prize away, enlisting the help of the winds to whip it from his fingers, urging the rain to loosen his grip so that it would slide away, but to no avail. The herder was resolute and strong, and accustomed to the ferocity of nature. She even asked the sun to turn up the heat, to scorch the mirror from his hands, but the boy would sooner burn than give it up.

Eventually she turned to her son, the god of love, Cupid.

"Steal it for me, I beg you!"

Cupid sneered. He was tired of his mother's demands, but being dutiful he reluctantly obeyed.

"I will try, but I cannot promise a result."

And so the cherub took to the air, materialising in a matter of seconds before the boy's eyes.

"I have come for my mother's mirror," he said without introduction. "You must surely see that it is magic, and that you cannot keep it. I will return it to her now, and that will be the end of the matter."

But the boy held on, pressing the mirror to his chest, and wrapping his arms around it to display ownership.

"Give it to me!" Cupid cried and reached for the lad's arms, but he was quick and could dodge the blows.

His age and agility made it easy for him to escape the god's clutches, darting swiftly to the left or right depending on the attack. However, he hadn't accounted for the rough ground at his feet, which caught on his sandal causing him to trip. The mirror trembled beneath his grip. He tried desperately to hold on, but it was already in the air, and while Cupid attempted to grasp it, his stubby fingers would not stretch. The object fell and smashed upon the stony soil. Thousands of tiny fragments of glass splayed in every direction. They looked like glittering jewels peeping from the cracks and crevices.

For a moment it seemed that time stood till, as god and youth gazed in silence at the ground. The magic mirror was no more, but something else was growing in the place of each delicate shard: a tiny piece of enchantment in the form of a bell-shaped bloom. With bright green leaves and lavender blue nodding heads, the flower clustered together and spread like a carpet through the Mediterranean. Those who saw it would stop and stare, and in that moment be reminded of the beauty of nature, and feel grateful to be alive. They saw the essence of joy reflected back at them through the flowers' delightful charm, like an everlasting mirror, and a source of divine love.

## RITUAL TO BOOST CONFIDENCE AND SELF-LOVE

Bellflowers are a low-maintenance plant and can grow in tricky habitats with dry, rocky soil. Like this joyous flower you can also bloom with the right amount of light and love.

*You will need: An image of Bellflowers in bloom, and a mirror.*

- Close your eyes and bring to mind the image of the Bellflowers (perhaps use the one in this book). They may be small and delicate, but they are also beautiful and grow in abundance. Reflect upon their beauty.
- Open your eyes and stare at your own reflection in the mirror.
- Make eye contact with yourself and smile. See the beauty of your face as you relax and become more confident.
- Know that like the Bellflower, you also bloom when given love.
- Say, "I blossom and flourish, I radiate beauty."

# BUTTERCUP
## *Ranunculus repens*

Buttercups are a creeping perennial with bright yellow glossy flowers shaped like tiny cups. Each bloom has at least five petals.

**FLOWER MEANING** Associated with childish fun, youthfulness, joy, and delight.

**FOLKLORE ORIGIN** England

## THE MISER'S GOLD

It was a spring day like any other. The season, which had long been in slumber beneath winter's gnarly blanket, was stirring. The soil, once cracked and covered in icy rivets, had now slackened, quenched by a recent downpour. The wildlife was awakening. Birds chirruped in the trees, and the tiny scamper of furry mammals could be felt as they tapped upon the earth.

Such a beautiful day made no difference to the miser. He was known for his grumpiness, as much as his greed. His lumbering form was a common sight shambling over hill and dale, making his way to and from the market with a hefty sack of treasure in his grasp. Never one to share his stash or store it, for fear that it would be stolen, he kept it with him at all times. No wonder then that carrying the weight of his wealth upon his back had given him a permanent stoop.

On this day, he was doing more of the same. Trudging from place to place, unaware of the beauty that accompanied his journey. Most gave the miser a wide berth. He was not a man to exchange pleasantries with, and if you did make that mistake, you'd regret taking the time. But those of a fey persuasion are never deterred by the bluntness of humankind. Such mercurial souls see it as something of a challenge to help us see the error of our ways. With a sprinkling of magic and some mischief thrown in, they'll do their best to lift the mood, and spread some joy. But be warned, should you cross or offend them, you'll likely feel the nip of fairy trickery at your heels. Perhaps the miser thought he was above such enchantments, being rich in other ways. Who knows?

And so it was that when the sprites sprang from the undergrowth and yelled, "Halloo!" with gusto, the miser jumped in his skin. He was unamused.

"Get out of my way, fools!" yelled the miser. "I have no time for this."

"And why be that?" asked the small sprite. "It seems to me you have all the time in the world."

The miser frowned. "You know nothing about me."

"Ah, I beg to differ. Let me introduce myself," the sprite said as he hoisted his red cap from his head and bowed low.

"GET OUT OF MY WAY!" the miser roared.

"He's very rude!" chimed in one of the other sprites.

"Perhaps it's that heavy sack he carries," said another. "It makes him sore and bristly."

"The sack is mine! Get your hands away from it," the miser snarled.

"Ooooh," said the first sprite, suddenly intrigued, "Methinks you have some gold in there! Perhaps you'd like to share your wealth with us?"

"I don't share what's mine with anyone!"

The sprite chuckled, "Yes, we thought as much. But have you considered what it would be like to be free of it all? How light you would feel without that heavy sack upon your shoulders?"

The miser strode forward, knocking the sprite to the floor with a swipe of his enormous hands. "I don't want to. It's mine. Now go away!"

And with that, he blundered forward, trampling through the wildflowers as he went. It's safe to assume that the miser thought that was the end of that. He had seen them off, and they would never bother him again, but what he failed to realize was that the sprites had already played their trick. When the miser hadn't been looking one of them had cut an opening in his sack, a hole just big enough for the nuggets of gold to fall in clumps to the ground. Bit by glittering bit, they leaked in a trail up the hillside, in between the flattened grass. They looked like jewels.

It was only when the miser reached the top of the hill, that he suddenly realized how different he felt, how his arms swung freely, and his joints bounced with a lightness that he had not experienced in a long time. His back, so set in a hunch, loosened, and with a deep breath he was able to straighten and tilt his head upward. "Why is this?" he wondered, believing he had been blessed by the gods with a different kind of fortune, and then it dawned upon him. He clasped what was left of his sack. The saggy material hung empty over his shoulder. The gold all gone.

"Filthy fairies!" he raged, and it was then that he saw the nuggets twinkling from the hillside below him. Turning on his heel, he made his way back down in the hope he could salvage his treasure, but he wasn't used to being without the weight of his sack, and he tumbled forward. Head over heels he fell, rolling down the hill at such a speed that he could not grasp the gold. And as he passed each piece, it transformed into a tiny five-petaled flower, with a cup-shaped bloom. More and more clusters formed, until the entire valley was covered with Buttercups. As for the miser, he eventually reached the bottom, and while he was sore and somewhat embarrassed, he also felt something else. Something he had not felt since he was a child. He opened his mouth, and instead of growling, or howling, he began to laugh. He laughed and laughed until he cried, and then he laughed some more. And when the laughter subsided, he returned to the top of the hill, and he rolled down again!

The sprites chuckled as they watched from a distance. "See, I told you," said the smallest of the group. "There's a child in all of us that wants to be free." And so upon that extraordinary spring day the golden Buttercup was born—a playful symbol synonymous with fun and youthfulness, and a reminder that true wealth only comes from joy.

## RITUAL TO FEEL REFRESHED AND JOYFUL

Buttercups grow in abundance in the wild, and it can be easy to dismiss their loveliness, and even consider them weeds. Take a moment to appreciate their natural wonder and recharge body and mind.

*You will need: Access to Buttercups growing in the wild, and a small bottle of water.*

- Sit by a patch of Buttercups and take in their beauty.
- Notice their golden glow, and how they give off light, despite being small in size.
- Relax your body, and let your shoulders fall back and chest soften.
- Draw a long slow breath in through your nose and release it slowly through the mouth. Take your time as you exhale and repeat this breathing cycle for a couple of minutes.
- As you inhale imagine you are being infused with the flower's golden light. Feel it filling up your chest with warmth.
- As you exhale, release any tension that you have been holding onto.
- To finish, take a sip of water, and sprinkle the rest over the flowers.

# PANSY
## *Viola tricolor var. hortensis*

Pansies are a small perennial with rounded leaves at the base and heart-shaped petals which overlap, and come in a range of color combinations.

**FLOWER MEANING** Associated with kindness, honesty, and loyalty.

**FOLKLORE ORIGIN** Germany

## THE SWEETEST SACRIFICE

Back when the Universe decided to take a lump of floating rock and turn it into a place where life could grow, everything was new and emerging. The seas were settling into their shape upon the Earth, learning to go with the flow of the tide. The trees which had sprouted from the tiniest saplings were finally branching out, stretching as far as the eye could see. The elements were testing their powers, the wind and rain battling for supremacy, while the sun languished in the sky, enjoying the spectacle below. The globe and all that lived upon it was finding their feet, and ultimately flourishing. And so it was that the flowers too, were discovering their unique beauty.

From the tall willowy blooms that swayed in the breeze, to the dainty flowers that preferred to stay close to the ground, they all had their assets which they used to gain favor. Among the smaller blooms